Are You Taking Me Home Now?
Adventures with Dad

by Karen Molenaar Terrell

In loving memory of Moz,
and for Dad - my hero.

I'm two years old. I'm at Black Lake with Mom and Dad. I decide to go exploring. I venture out into the lake. Up to my knees. Up to my waist. There's a drop off. I take one step too many and go under. I am not happy about this. I try to turn around, but my feet aren't taking me anywhere. I open my mouth to holler, but water fills my mouth and only burbles come out. I'm angry now. I am not having any fun here. Suddenly I see two big feet - one on either side of me - and I am yanked out of the water by my pony tail. I come out of the water screaming and turn in strong arms to look up at my savior. It is my handsome father, smiling at me. He is my hero. I know I'm safe now.

Spring

I am four years old. Dad has taken me to Mount Rainier to do my first scramble up Pinnacle Peak. He has a rope tied around my waist as I climb with hands and feet to the top - learning how to balance, how to pull and push myself up the rock face. I am smiling with the joy of adventure.

"People Aren't Giving Me a Straight Answer"
March 4, 2017

I stop in to see Dad and he asks how Mom is doing. I tell him Mom is fine. He looks at me, skeptically, and says, "It feels like people aren't giving me a straight answer to this question." Dad does not like it when people lie to him. He is very sharp. He is also profoundly hard-of-hearing - so I get close to his ear and tell him Mom passed. He asks me what I said. I tell him I love him and hug him and leave.

I come back later with a new pair of pants for him. Mary from *The Mountaineers* is there and Dad is busy at the dining room table drawing a picture of Rainier on some watercolor paper she's brought him. He asks how Mom is. I tell him fine. I ask him how he is, and he says he'd be happier if he knew how Mom was. I ask him if he'd like me to write him a note about Mom and he nods his head yes. I write: "Daddy, Mom passed on peacefully in her sleep at my house last week. She loved you very much. She still loves you. She knows you love her, too. We all love you, Daddy. You're not alone. We're all here for you."

He asks how "the boys" are doing. I say the boys are doing fine and want him to be happy.

I write to him that he was able to see Mom before they brought her to my house. I tell him an attendant wheeled him up to Mom's room so he could say good-bye. The attendant said it was the most beautiful thing he'd ever seen.

Mary and I are hugging him and he's holding my hand. I find a paper napkin and dab tears off the end of his nose. He asks if Mom died in pain, and I say no, she died peacefully at my house. I tell him I was sleeping on the couch next to her bed when she passed. He wants to know what she died of, and I tell him her heart had gotten tired and stopped.

I tell him about the memorial celebration scheduled for her in a few weeks, and he nods his head that he wants to come.

I ask him what I can do to help, what he wants to do now. He says he wants to go to bed. So Mary and I help him get back to his room. He tells me he loves me before I leave.

I think he might ask again – and I think we're going to have to continue to be truthful with him, and help him get through this. He won't let us lie to him. He is very brave.

"I'll Be Around for a While"
March 6, 2017

I pick Dad up for an outing. He is brilliant. As we're driving through the Skagit countryside he looks around and says, "This is beautiful country. Low-lying hills and mountains beyond..." And then a little later he comments, "Human figures are very small in this landscape." And later still he says, "This area is an interesting mix of recreation, agriculture, and industry."

After our errands we go to the Farmhouse Inn for lunch. He tells me he misses Mom. I tell him I do, too. He says he had no idea she was so close to dying, but he thinks she might have known. I tell him that she knew. He nods his head, accepting this. I tell him I'm so glad I still have him - and... I wish I could describe clearly what he looks like at that moment - he looks like a weary and battle-worn noble Tolkien elf-king - white-haired, white-bearded - and he says, "I'll be around for a while, yet." And he says it in a way that... he's not bragging or showing bravado... he's comforting me. He's speaking fact.

Dad's New Friends
March 13, 2017

I stop in to see Dad in the hospital - he's looking much better.

After I visit Dad I go to his adult family home to check in with the care-givers there and give an update. And I love that place! I tell Erica, one of the care-givers, how Dad said he "didn't want to live with a bunch of old people" when we first moved him into a retirement place with Mom. I say that I bet he loves it in this home because there are usually young people in the house - grand-children and children of the care-givers - and Erica says her sons love Dad. She says Dad tells them about the expeditions he's been on and the places he's been and shares his adventures with the boys - and they sit there with their mouths open in awe and wonder, listening to him, and asking him questions. That tickles me. She says Dad asked her to get one of his books for him, and she reached down and pulled out *The Challenge of Rainier* from his little book case there - and he said, "That's a good one, isn't it?"

I love the friendships he's making in this place. They know him, and love him there, and that means everything to me.

When we brought Dad into the ER yesterday, one of the doctor's saw his name come up on the screen and immediately recognized it and said, "I'm going to take this one! I'm not giving him to these other Philistines who don't know who he is!" So that was cool - that this doctor who happened to be a climber saw Dad's name and instantly made a connection with him as someone he knew and admired.

As I drive home from the hospital, the rain pattering on the car - I just... I feel this sense of peace. I've been dealing with lots of "to-do" things the last few weeks - closing Mom and Dad's accounts, paying off their bills, talking to banks and lawyers, Veterans Administration folks, making decisions about finances and health care for my parents, hospital people, hospice people, hospice equipment people, funeral director, finding a new home for Dad, trying to put together a memorial celebration for Moz. And there's still more to do. But I find myself just letting go of all that for a bit. I come home and get a fire going in the woodstove; make a blackberry pie (it's in the oven as I type); put in *Guardians of the Galaxy*. The cat is asleep on the ottoman; the dog is asleep next to me on the couch. I enjoy these few hours of peace. I feel happy.

I am in the garden section in Fred Meyer's and I look around and think, "Oh, I should buy some flowers for Moz's deck... something that will attract the hummingbirds..." And then I remember.

"I'm Too Much Trouble"
March 15, 2017

Dad: You like to organize like my sister, Jo. But she was more serious. You're more fun. (*Thinking.*) Thank you for taking me to all these appointments. (*Thinking.*)You've spent your whole day with me.

Karen: We love you! We want to be here!

Dad: I'm too much trouble. (*Musing.*) I always knew Mom would go first. But I never knew I'd take it like this. (*Thinking.*) How many tears can a person cry? How long can a person cry? Where is the tear water stored? Is it stored somewhere in your head? (*Thinking.*) I could live here in this hospital room so long as I had company now and then. They're feeding me well here. (*More thinking.*) I've lost my brother, K, my sister, Jo, my wife, most of the friends from my generation...

"You're the Pretty One"
March 17, 2017

As Dad is sitting in the wheelchair, ready to be discharged from the hospital, one of the nursing attendants leans over and asks him if he remembers her from the day before. Dad nods his head yes, and then says, "You're the pretty one."

She sort of blushes, and starts laughing, and says, "No, no," all embarrassed. Dad sits there with a grin on his face.

When we go to pick Dad up we find out his clothes are lost somewhere between the Emergency Room and his current hospital room. We could write a report, we're told - but the chances of finding his clothes again aren't likely. My husband, Scott, asks me if Dad wore shoes into the hospital - and then I remember that Dad had worn those special sneakers we'd bought last year because Mom had so wanted him to have new sneakers on his feet. Those sneakers had sentimental value. I decide to go back to the ER and see what I can find out.

The nice lady at the desk makes a call, then another call, then a third call, and finally reaches someone who's going to look in the "locked cupboard" to see if his things are in there. Pretty soon a nurse comes around the corner and tells us his clothes weren't in the locked cupboard. She tells me to check the lost and found - and the lady at the desk tells her they have no lost and found. The nurse asks me what his shoes looked like - gray sneakers with white laces, I tell her - and she says, "I think I saw some sneakers back there... let me check..." And about five minutes later she comes back with a bag full of Dad's clothes - including the sneakers and INCLUDING THE ALPINE HAT FROM THE MATTERHORN WHICH HE WEARS EVERYWHERE AND WHICH I'D COMPLETELY FORGOTTEN ABOUT!!! Ohmygosh!!! That was a close call, my friends!!! I am so grateful to be able to put his Matterhorn hat back on his head, and his dashing gray sneakers back on his feet.

Something Kind of Wonderful
March 25, 2017

Something kind of wonderful happened this morning. I was waiting for my friend, Teresa, at the Fred Meyer eating area – Teresa was going to help me figure out what I needed to buy for the memorial celebration today – and this little family came in and sat down next to me – Mom with a baby, her daughter who'd just turned eight, other family members – and I started chatting with them – really neat people.

Pretty soon this man came in with a backpack and all kinds of bags hanging out of his pockets and out of his pack. I saw him trying to organize all his bags and was kind of intrigued by him.

Then Teresa came in – bringing all that wonderful energy with her – and I introduced her to my new friends sitting next to me. They started chatting, and I left them to go talk to the man with all the bags. I asked him if I could buy him a coffee at the Starbucks – and he asked me if I could maybe buy him a couple gift cards so he can buy food later. So I found the gift card rack and he picked out a Kroger's card for food, and a Starbucks card, and I went back to the cashier to buy it for him, and also to buy some drinks for Teresa and me. (Teresa didn't want me to buy her anything, until my new friend told her that I'm the boss today, and she has to do what I say.)

So we all got our drinks – the backpack man thanked me for the cards – he said he'd been having a really negative attitude about people up until then, and I'm making him feel better about life. Teresa turned to him and said, "Do you want to know why she bought you those cards today? Her mom died and today is the celebration for her mom, and she's buying you those cards in honor of her mom who was the most loving person in the world." And as Teresa told him this, I realized that it's true. Moz taught me to watch out for people, and to do what I could to help. And the idea of that brought sweet tears to my eyes.

So the man thanked me and we parted ways, and Teresa and I went back to our table, and my new friend, Ella, thanked me for taking care of the man with the backpack. Just the fact that she noticed the exchange with the backpack-man really touched my heart.

And THEN we found out we are both of the same political persuasion. And now I have a new FB friend.

Moz's celebration was wonderful. There was music and laughter and more music and laughter and sweet friendship. I brought her shoes to the celebration and put them in the front with all the flowers. It made me smile to see them up there.

"I Grew This Beard out for Her"
March 28, 2017

When I stop by to see Dad today he looks up and sees me and there are tears in his eyes. He's remembered that Moz is gone. He says, "I grew this beard out for her, and now she'll never see it." I give him a napkin to wipe his tears and he says, "Tears are a wonderful release."

I bring out the album of photos from Moz's memorial service - he doesn't remember being there - and I show him himself in the pictures, surrounded by his family and old friends - he recognizes every face - and he says, "I have a lot of good friends." And then he points to himself in the picture and says, "There's a good-looking Dutchman."

It Was Very Sweet
April 1, 2017

Scott and I brought Dad over for a couple hours today. On the way over, I was sitting behind him on the back seat and he reached back for my hand and brought it to his chest and squeezed it and kept hanging onto it. It was very sweet. He worked a little bit on his painting ("Have I been working on this one since before Christmas?") And then sat next to me on the couch and leaned his head against mine and sort of dozed while a nature program played on *Netflix*. It reminded me of when the sons would nap with me in front of the TV when they were little.

"We Are a Good Father-Daughter Team"
April 24, 2017

Karen: I'm happy just to be with you.

Dad: That's the best thing to hear. We are a good father-daughter team.

Karen: Yes, we are.

I take Dad to the social security office to change his address. When it's our turn he has a hard time getting up from his seat. I reach out to help him, and immediately someone comes from the left, someone comes from the right, and the security guard rushes over - everyone ready to help Dad get to his feet. People always want to help when they have the chance.

Flowers for Our Friend
May 12, 2017

The flower place I use every year to send flowers to Moz on Mother's Day emailed me to let me know about the special deals it has right now. I let my friends know about this. They know my mom passed away at the end of February, and I figured they'd know what that email notification from the flower place meant to me. Several of my friends suggested I think of someone else to send flowers to this year. I really liked the idea of that a lot.

So today my friend, Laurie – a woman my mom loved dearly – received Mother's Day flowers. In my mind Laurie received those flowers from both Moz and me. I imagine Moz smiling. I know she would have really been tickled by Laurie getting those flowers.

"The Past and the Present Are Coming Together"
May 15, 2017

Dad: Where have you been? Are we going to your house for Christmas dinner? It's Christmas Eve, you know.

Karen: No, it's May, and you're going to be 99 in a month.

Dad: Oh. I used to be so sharp. Now I'm losing everything. The past and the present are coming together...

Karen: I sure love you.

Dad: I love you, too. (*Pause.*) You remember you used to tell me you hated me?

Karen: I never told you I hated you. I've always loved you.

Dad: Oh.

Today's conversation was a hard one for me.

"Are You Taking Me Home Now?"
May 19, 2017

Dad: Are you taking me home now?
Karen: Daddy, you are home.
Dad: I am? (*Surprised.*) When did I buy this one?
(*I'm laughing so hard all I can do is hug Dad.*)
Dad: What's happening this weekend?
(*I don't know and shrug to indicate I have no clue.*)

An animated Charles Schultz "Peanuts" cartoon is on the television. Dad and Charles Schultz had met and become friends at some point.

I write a note to Dad: Remember when you met Charles Schultz?

Dad: Yeah. (*Nods head.*) I wonder if he'll be at the party this weekend. He probably has a lot of parties to go to, though.

"I Wouldn't Mind"
May 22, 2017

Karen: Daddy, do you want to go for a drive?

Dad: I wouldn't mind.

(*In the car.*)

Dad: Thank you for taking me for a drive. You're a good daughter.

Karen: It's my pleasure.

Dad: Do you prefer to call me "Dad" or "Father"?

Karen: I call you "Daddy."

(*We turn into the Sisters Espresso. Dad recognizes this as the place where I buy him root beer floats.*)

Dad: Oh good! This is exactly what we need right now!

(*Back on the road - Dad's got his root beer float and I have my lavender ice tea.*)

Dad: This is the longest time I haven't seen Mom. I think she's in Kansas City... or somewhere in the Midwest... helping the government.

Karen: I know she's doing a good job.

(*We reach the Chuckanut Hills.*)

Dad: I used to do water rights surveys out here when I worked for the USGS.

Karen: That was a fun part of your job, wasn't it?

Dad: Yes. I always took little detours when I went on these survey trips. (*He looks around and studies the landscape.*) This is a beautiful part of the world.

(*We've gotten to Fairhaven now.*)

Dad: I wonder how many places are called Fairhaven. It's a good name. It has a happy sound to it.

(*We get all the way to Boulevard Park. For some reason, every single parking space is taken today.*)

Dad: Are we going to park here and walk around?

Karen: There's no parking today. We'll try to do that another day.

(*Dad nods his head in understanding.*)

As we drive up from the park I spot my old friend, Darryl - Darryl and I made acquaintance on the boardwalk several years ago when we saw each other taking photos and struck up conversation. In the course of our conversation we'd realized that Darryl's Aunt Gladdie was one of Mom and Dad's good friends in a town three hours to the south.

I stop now and roll down the window and introduce Dad to Darryl - and try to explain that Darryl's aunt is Gladdie. I'm not sure Dad can hear what I'm saying and I'm not sure he understands what is going on, but he smiles and shakes Darryl's hand and we move on.

A minute later he asks, "Was he related to Gladdie in some way?" I tell him he's Gladdie's nephew. Dad asks me how I discovered this - "Did he have a sign on him that said he was Gladdie's nephew?" he joked. I explain how Darryl and I had met by chance and discovered we had his Aunt Gladdie in common. Dad nods. In his world, this kind of coincidence is probably perfectly normal. He knows a lot of people.

(*We head back down Chuckanut.*)

Dad: Do you take a lot of drives with Mom?

Karen: Yes. (*I take my late mother on all my drives with me.*) But I like taking drives with you, too.

Dad: We don't talk much. (*I can tell he's thinking about his hearing problem.*)

Karen: No, but it doesn't matter.

Dad: It doesn't matter because we're with each other.

Karen: Right! (*Smiling.*)

We get back to his home. He has a hard time getting in and out of the car these days. He tries to shift his feet out of the car and onto the pavement. This is hard work. He sighs and laughs and looks up at me.

Dad: These days it's just hard getting up the energy to get out of the car.

(*I can tell he's gathering his energy to lift himself out of the seat and I reach under his armpits to help him. "One-two-three!" And he's up!*)

Dad: Thank you for the drive today.

Karen: It was fun, wasn't it?

Dad: Yes, I enjoyed it very much.

Karen: I love you.
Dad: I love you, too.

"I Don't Want to Run Errands"
May 29, 2017

Dad: Let's head out into the open countryside, head towards the coast.

Karen: Let's do it!

Dad: I don't want to go into the city. I don't want to run errands with you.

(*I nod my head in understanding.*)

Dad: (*His voice cracking.*) I love you.

Karen: I love you, too.

Dad: It's nice that we have each other to love.

Karen: Yes, it is!

Dad: Thank you for including me when you take these drives. (*I smile - I take these drives FOR Dad.*)

I turn onto Samish Island Road, thinking maybe I'll go to Bayview State Park.

Dad: Have you ever been to that little island that's connected to the land?

Karen: Samish Island? Do you want to go there?

(*Dad nods his head, and I head out to do the loop around Samish Island.*)

Dad: Is Mom alive?

(*I shake my head no.*)

Dad: I had a dream that she'd died. (*He starts tearing up.)* I think I've already mourned her.

(*Dad's quiet for a bit. We've almost finished the Samish Island loop now.*)

Dad: Can we see Mount Rainier from here?

Karen: I think it's hidden behind those hills.

Dad: Let's go someplace where we can walk on a beach.

(*I head for Bayview State Park.*)

After parking, Dad and I make our way to a bench near the beach. When I'm getting Dad's walker out of the back of the car, I see the cans of root beer I put in there months ago - I'd bought them for Dad, and had forgotten about them. Now I grab one, join Dad on the bench, and hand the root beer to him. His face lights up and he smiles and takes it from me.

Dad: Do you ever dream about Mom?

Karen: Yes. I had a dream that she was sitting on the top bed of a bunk bed, dangling her feet over the edge. She had a happy, mischievous smile on her face. There was an open casket on the bed behind her. She said, "I'm done with this!" and hopped down. I felt like she was done with the whole dead-thing, and was happy. Have you had a dream about Mom?

Dad: Yes. I dreamed she died.

Karen: She loved you, and loves you very much.

Dad: She was such a wonderful person.

Karen: Yes, she is!

(*Dad and I are quiet for a while, just enjoying the sunshine.*)

Dad: This is nice here. I'm glad we made this stop. That's a nice, gentle breeze. It smells like saltwater. (*He belches and laughs at his own belch.*)

When we get back in the car, Dad says he had a dream where he had to fart once, but there was no place to fart. He starts laughing - cracking himself up. I'm laughing, too. Then Dad asks, "Do you and Mom have a lot of nice conversations?" And I tell him that we do.

As we're heading back to Dad's home, he turns his head and points, "That would make a happy picture! That house all covered in flowers! But I don't have my camera with me..." I turn the car around and head back to the flower-bedecked house, and get out my camera for Dad to snap a photo.

We get back to his home, and Dad doesn't recognize it at first - he has moved three times in the last year, and it's all a little confusing. I explain that their last home couldn't take Mom and him back when Mom got sick. And then when Mom passed, we had to find another home for Dad. I tell Dad that I felt that Mom had directed us to this place - a place with hummingbird feeders and cats and dogs. Dad asks, "So Mom knows these people then?" And I think about this, and then nod my head yes. (*I believe Mom does know these people, even if they never actually met in the person.*)

Dad gets back in the house and doesn't recognize anything. I ask him if he wants to go to his room - and he asks, "I have a room here?" I point the way, and once he enters he says, "Oh! I remember this place now!" He sees his paintings on the walls, and pictures of his friends and family. He realizes he's home. He starts grinning at himself and says, "I've been thanking these people for allowing me to stay here."

Dad points to a book by Leif Whittaker about Leif's father, Jim. "I think I got that book for Christmas." I tell him that I think Jim Whittaker gave him that book when he came to visit him here. "Jim visited me here?!" Yes, I tell him, also his friends Rick and Cindy, and Tom Hornbein, and Mary from the Mountaineers. Dad is shaking his head in amazement now. He says, "The things I've forgotten would fill a book!"

Karen: Are you going to take a nap now?

Dad: Yes, I want to make that transition into the dream.

Karen: What dream is that?

Dad: (*Tearing up.*) The dream about the real world. (*And I know he's thinking about the world where Mom is still with him.*)

Karen: I love you, Dad.

Dad: I love you, Karen.

"Would It Help to Let Them Know I'm 98?"
June 5, 2017

I enjoyed a most excellent day. I took a walk around Lake Padden - and it was green and ferny and mossy and perfect - with that wonderful smell of a living lake wafting off the water. Then I picked up Dad for a drive. Along the way we stopped at the bank to do some business. I brought a pad and pen with me so I could let Dad know what was going on without having to yell in his ear.

Laura, my favorite bank person at Dad's bank, brought us back into her office. I wrote on the pad for Dad: "Laura is awesome!" and then focused on Laura. I wasn't paying attention to what Dad was doing, but when I looked at the pad, he'd written, "So am I." I looked at him, and he was grinning at me. He is a character. It took a while for Laura's computer to do what she needed it to do and she explained that the system was up-dating. So I wrote on the pad: "Their system is up-dating." When I looked back at the pad a few minutes later Dad had written: "Would it help to let them know that I'm 98?" I started laughing with Dad and said, "Come on - the man is 98, for crying out loud - he doesn't have all day!" Then I wrote on the pad, "You're going to be 99 in two weeks!" And he made that "Really?!!" expression.

After the bank business we went to the ice cream place in LaConner, and Dad had his usual - a vanilla cone. We sat under the shade of the table bumbershoot and ate our ice creams and smiled back and forth at each other. Then it was back in the car and back through the Skagit farmland and back to Dad's home - where we told each other we loved each other and bid good bye.

When I got home I hopped on my bike and had a quick ride to the post office, and then came back home to Dr. Strange on Netflex and avocado on toast.

A perfect jewel of a day.

"I've Been Sitting Here for Hours"
June 7, 2017

I stop by to see Dad after school. He's sitting on the patio, listening to Allison Lickley singing "Mountains" - his feet propped up on at ottoman, looking entirely at peace. He says, "This is nice. The temperature is perfect. I've been sitting out here for hours." It is one of those magic times in life when everything is still and calm and beautiful and the very air seems filled with joy and love.

Dad is living the good life.

"Are You Taking Me to Jo's?"
June 12, 2017

Karen: Do you want to go for a drive today?

Dad: Are you taking me to Jo's?

Karen: Jo who?

Dad: My sister.

(*Pause while I figure out what direction to go with this.*)

Karen: Dad, your sister has been gone a long time now.

Dad: No... (*Reads the expression on my face.*) Why didn't anyone tell me?

Karen: You knew, Dad. You just forgot. It's okay. Do you want to go for a drive?

Dad: Alright.

This time I decide to head east towards the mountains. We go through Lyman - I point out my old house there and Dad remembers taking "the boys" down to the Skagit River for a walk. He says, "I used to walk around this neighborhood." And I tell him that yes, he did.

Dad, the geologist: (*Looking out the window at the Skagit River.*) That's a big river. I think it's the biggest river in western Washington. It gets a lot of its water from Canada.

Karen: Isn't it beautiful?

Dad: Yes, it is.

Dad: When did Jo die?

Karen: Years ago. (*Pause.*) Dad, how much older was Jo than you?

Dad: She was two and a half years older than me.

Karen: You're almost 99 now. How old would Jo be if she was still alive?

Dad: (*Puzzling it out.*) She'd be 101.

Karen: She'd be really old, wouldn't she?

(*Dad nods his head, understanding.*)

Karen: She lived a really long time. Into her 90s.

Dad: K probably knows about this.

Karen: Remember K passed on before Jo?

(*Dad nods his head, remembering now.*)

Dad: I wonder how many of the people I used to work with think I'm dead now.

Karen: You've lost a lot of family and friends... Kurt is gone now... (*I bring up Kurt's name because I know Dad tried to mail him a letter the other day.*)

Dad: Kurt's gone? I haven't heard from Kurt's wife for a while. She's probably gone, too. (*She is.*)

(*I stop to buy him a milkshake at the Dairy Queen in Sedro-Woolley. Dad orders his usual: vanilla.*)

Dad: "Chocolate just tastes like burnt vanilla to me."

(*As we're heading back towards his home, Dad asks me the question I was hoping I'd be able to avoid today.*)

Dad: Is Mom dead?

Karen: Yes.

Dad: Is she? (*His eyes tear up, but he doesn't seem really surprised this time.*) I'm a widower then. (*He takes a big suck on his milkshake.*)

(*I bring him back to his home.*)

Dad: "Is this my permanent residence now?"

(*I nod yes.*)

Dad: How are the boys taking Mom's death?

Karen: It's hard. But we're all doing fine. I sure love you, Dad.

Dad: I love you, too.

Karen: We're in this together, Dad. You're not alone.

(*Dad nods his head, and squeezes my hand.*)

Summer

The summer after I graduate from high school —about ten years after the Watts Riots — I travel with Dad to California. Dad had grown up in Los Angeles, and he wants to revisit his old neighborhood and see his childhood home once again. As we drive the streets to his old home, I notice that we are the only white faces in a several-mile radius.

Dad pulls up in front of a little house, and his face lights up — "This was my home!" he says, getting out of the car. I follow him to the front door, where an African-American woman wearing a house-dress and a really surprised look on her face, appears. Dad explains that he grew up in this house and asks if he can come in and take a look around and go out into the backyard where he played as a child. The woman smiles graciously and opens her door for us and allows us into her home.

I follow Dad through the house and out into the backyard where there is still the avocado tree he remembers from his childhood. He looks around, says it seems smaller than he remembered it, and starts talking about the happy years he spent in this yard as a child. He goes back through the house, shakes the woman's hand and thanks her for letting him re-visit his old home. Still looking kind of surprised to find these friendly white people traipsing through her house, she smiles back at Dad, and tells him he's welcome and it's no problem at all.

A block or so later Dad pulls into a gas station to fill the tank up, and a black attendant comes out to help us. He has the same surprised look on his face as the woman in Dad's old house. He smiles, and fills up our tank for us, and, as we're ready to leave, says in a friendly way, a big smile on his face, "Come back again!"

Every time I think of this trip through that neighborhood in Los Angeles I start grinning. I'm pretty sure we are the only white people in years who have come nonchalantly driving through that section of Los Angeles. I remember the surprised hospitality of the gas station attendant and the woman living in Dad's old house, and it fills me up with a kind of joy. I remember my dad — totally oblivious to the fact that he was in a part of Los Angeles that most white people might find threatening — happily traveling down "Memory Lane" - shaking hands with the woman in his old house, greeting the gas station attendant with an open, natural smile – and it makes me really proud to be his daughter.

"I Was Just Thinking About You"
June 30, 2017

I run a few errands and end up at Dad's home about 11:00. Sometimes that's too early and he's still in bed, but today he's up and just finishing breakfast. I ask him if he wants to go for a drive today and he says yes, he would.

Dad: Let's head for Edison.

(*I head for Edison.*)

Dad: (*Smiling.*) I was just thinking about you and taking a drive with you when you showed up.

Karen: I'm so glad!

(*As we're driving out of Burlington, Dad points to Burlington Hill.*)

Dad: If I lived next to that hill, I'd climb it every week.

(*I stop at Sister's Espresso for his root beer float and my lavender lemonade.*)

Dad: Thank you. Did you feel happy when you moved up here?

Karen: Yes, I did.

Dad: This is beautiful country.

Karen: Yes, it is.

(*We drive through Edison.*)

Dad: This is a nice little town.

(*We leave Edison and head into the country. Dad is looking towards the refinery stacks in Anacortes.*)

Dad: You can always tell when it's good weather by looking at the stacks. The smoke is blowing southward.

(*We arrive in LaConner - I have to pick up Dad's mail from his old home, the LaConner Retirement Inn.*)

Dad: Would you like to live here?

(*I'm not sure if Dad remembers living here from March 2016 to Mom's passing in February 2017, so I answer his question carefully.*)

Karen: Yes. This is a nice little town. I have a friend who lives right there in that house. (*I point to Debbie's house.*) What about you? Would you like living here?

(Dad nods his head and says yes. I stop at the LaConner Retirement Inn to get his mail. I pick up his mail and get back in the car. Dad is napping, but wakes up when I open the door. I drive through LaConner, past the places where Dad and Moz and I sometimes ate and walked, waiting to see if Dad recognizes where we are. As we're about to leave LaConner...)

Dad: What is the name of this little town?

Karen: This is LaConner.

(We drive out of LaConner and head towards Conway. I see Mount Baker above green fields, and point to it.)

Karen: See Baker, Dad?

Dad: Yes. It's faded, though.

Karen: It's kind of hazy out. Here - try my sunglasses.

(Dad puts my sunglasses on.)

Dad: *(Smiling.)* Oh! Yeah! That's better!

(I snap a photo, and pull back onto the road.)

Dad: Thank you for giving me these brief respites from my life. I really enjoy these drives.

Karen: I do, too, Dad.

(We pass through Conway and I get onto Old Highway 99 to snap some photos of Baker. I especially like the image of the little red sheds in the green fields in front of Baker. I show Dad the pictures I've taken.)

Dad: These would be good for watercolors. I'd get rid of the little red sheds, though.

(I smile, and tell him I'll print off copies of the pictures and he can make watercolors from them if he wants. We've been gone an hour and a half now, and it's time to bring Dad home. We head back for Burlington. I pull up in front of his door.)

Dad: Are we getting out here?

Karen. Yup. You're home!

Dad: Okay.

(We disembark and Melissa helps Dad up the stairs and into the living room. Dad settles himself into his lounger.)

Dad: Are you going now?

Karen: Yes. I love you, Dad.

Dad: I love you, too.

"So Shall We Go for a Drive?"
July 3, 2017

Dad says he misses Mom. He wishes he could have said good-bye to her. I tell him he did. He says he doesn't remember and asks if anyone took a picture of him saying good-bye to her. I show him pictures from the memorial service. He asks if he controlled himself at the service, and I tell him he did - he did a good job. He's relieved. He sees a picture of my brother, Pete, giving his talk at the service and asks if Peter controlled himself, and I say he did. He asks about Peter and my other brother, David, and I tell him they were just up last week to celebrate his birthday, and he says, "Oh, yeah," and nods his head.

Dad: So shall we go for a drive?

(*Usually I'm the one who asks Dad if he wants to go for a drive, and it tickles me that he took the initiative today.*)

Dad: (*As we're heading out of town...*) What do you think of wall beds?

(*I'm not sure I heard him right.*)

Karen: What do YOU think of wall beds?

Dad: They take up a lot of room on the wall.

(*We stop at the espresso stand and Dad says that today he'd like a vanilla shake, instead of his usual root beer float. I hand him his shake.*)

On the way up Chuckanut Drive, I've decided that maybe I'll bring Dad to my home and see if he wants to paint - he hasn't done that for a while. I'm also going to try to find a picture of Dad and Moz together in the hospital - it doesn't even matter if it's the last time Moz was in the hospital - I have a vague recollection of a photo where Dad's holding Moz's hand during one of her hospital visits, and I think that might work. I'll also print out pictures for Dad from our drive of the other day.

I bring out Dad's watercolors, brushes, and the painting he's been working on since before Christmas.

Dad: I've been working on this one forever. I may work on it forever, whether I want to or not.

Dad: Do you paint?
Karen: I paint a little, but I'm not as good as you.
Dad: Do you do watercolors?
Karen: Yes.
Dad: I prefer watercolors. I don't like using oils.
Karen: Watercolors are more subtle, aren't they?
(*Dad nods.*)

I go upstairs to print out the pictures for Dad - I find the one where Dad is holding Moz's hand in the hospital a year ago. I'm hoping he'll accept this as a picture of him saying good-bye to her. I bring the prints down and share them with Dad. He looks at each picture and nods his head. He sees the one where he's holding Mom's hand and accepts that he was saying good-bye to her in this one.

Dad works on his painting for an hour or so. It's peaceful and quiet while I watch him work - and there's something so beautiful about these moments together that I feel myself start to tear up. It occurs to me that I'm with a living piece of history here - a man who was born at the end of World War I and carries around almost a century of memories in him. I picture that noble, old knight guarding The Holy Grail in that Indiana Jones movie, and think, "That part could have been played by Daddy."

After an hour Dad is starting to look tired. Painting is hard work - it takes a lot of concentration.

Karen: Are you ready to go home for a nap?
Dad: Not necessarily. (*I can tell he doesn't want to leave, but I also know that our window of time is running out here - soon he'll need to be back near his bed and his bathroom. Dad maybe realizes this, too. He looks at his painting, and then starts to tidy up his brushes and paints. He puts on his hat. It's time to go.*)

I help him get back into the car - he looks like he's situated - and I go inside to get my sunglasses. When I come outside Dad is lying next to the car on the concrete.

Karen: Oh, Daddy. Crap. What happened?
Dad: (*Calmly.*) I fell getting into the car.

Karen: (*I'm trying to assess what we're dealing with here. Dad appears to be unhurt. He's looking straight up into the sun, though - so I put my sunglasses on him.*) Do you have any ideas how we can get you back up?

Dad: Well, maybe I could roll over into the grass, and then you could help me up from there.

(*It strikes me as weird and kind of funny how calm we both are about our situation. I find myself starting to chuckle, and Dad chuckles along with me. Suddenly our neighbor, Dan, appears next to us, ready to help. He is, to my mind, God-sent.*)

Dad: The car door's in the way. I can't stretch my legs out.

(*Dan and I lift Dad's shoulders and pull him a couple feet so he can stretch out.*)

Dad: I could just lay here for a while. This is comfortable.

Dan: No, we can't leave you here like this. (*Dan gets his hands behind Dad's shoulders and lifts him up and steers him into the car.*)

Dad: (*To Dan...*) Thank you.

We arrive back at his home and get him into the house. I let everyone know that Dad had a fall under my watch - I'm feeling guilty about this - but I'm assured by the kind people there that these things happen.

Karen: Well, Dad, we survived another adventure. No more falls, okay?

Dad: (*Smiles.*) Okay.

"I'm a Mixture of Both"
July 4, 2017

Scott calls from the supermarket to ask if there's anything he can bring home. I suggest that he stops by Dad's home to see if it might be a good time to bring him back to our house. I'm not sure if I'll be seeing Dad in the car when Scott pulls into the driveway - there are a lot of variables at play in determining whether Dad is up for a trip: Is he awake? Has he eaten? Has he used the bathroom, yet? How's he feeling? But the longer Scott is gone, the more hopeful I become that Dad will be coming back with him.

So I get the table prepared for Dad to work on his watercolor painting - bring out his paints, brushes, sponge, a jar filled with water, his latest painting - hoping he'll show up with Scott. And when Scott drives into the driveway with Dad sitting beside him in the car I feel my heart give a jump of joy. Oh goodie! Daddy is here!

When I open the car door for him, Dad is working to undo his seatbelt.

Dad: My seatbelt wasn't fastened. (*It was.*) I guess we need to go back and do it all over again (*he's smiling*).

He works his way out of the car, we give him his walker and he moves his way up the ramp to our front porch.

Dad: When did you put this ramp in?

Karen: When they had to bring Mom into the house on her hospital bed.

(*Dad nods, but I'm not sure he hears or understands what I said.*)

He goes right to the table and sits down in front of his painting. He chooses a brush and gets to work.

It's quiet, but for the ticking of the clock, and the sound of Dad swishing his brush around in the water and on the paper.

Karen: Who are you most like - your dad or your mom?
Dad: I'm a mixture of both.
Karen: Who do you look like?
Dad: I look more like my mom. K looked more like my dad. Jo looked a lot like Mom.

Karen: Your mother's face was rounder. Your father's face had higher cheekbones.

(*Dad nods his head.*)

Karen: You get your creativity from your mom?

(*Dad nods his head.*)

Karen: And you get your sense of humor from your dad, maybe?

Dad: No. Dad never laughed at farts - he just made them. (*Dad starts laughing.*)

Karen: Who do you get your humor from then?

Dad: My brother. My brother and I got our humor from each other.

Karen: That's the way it is with my sons. They'll be sitting in the back seat of the car when I'm driving and I'll be listening in to their conversation and laughing so hard I have tears running down my face.

Dad: You laugh about what they're saying?

Karen: Yes. They crack me up. (*Dad starts chuckling.*)

Dad: Are your boys close?

Karen: Yes. They're good friends.

Dad: Are you and Peter and David close?

Karen: Yes.

(*Dad settles in to working on his painting now.*)

Karen: Who do I look like?

Dad: (*Looks up at me and studies my face.*) You look like my dad.

Karen (*Something has just occurred to me - I don't think I've ever thought of this before...*) Dad, did you ever meet your grandparents?

Dad: No, I never met the Dutchies.

Karen: Did your mom and dad ever go back to the Netherlands and see their parents again?

Dad: No.

Karen: Wow. That was really brave of them to come all the way over here and never see their parents again.

Dad: (*Trying to remember...*) Did you ever meet your grandparents?

Karen: All my grand-parents were gone before I was born, except Mom's mom.

(*Dad nods his head, remembering now.*)

Karen: But my sons got to meet their grandparents, and I'm really glad about that.

(*Dad nods his head, agreeing.*)

I feel enclosed in a bubble of love: Dad's sitting to the right of me, quietly working on his painting; Scott's sitting to the left of me, quietly working on his photos; Clara Kitty is sitting on my shoulder, purring. The feeling of love is so deep and powerful, I feel myself tearing up. I can feel Moz in the room with us.

Karen: Are you almost done with the painting now?

Dad: (*Looks up and smiles.*) Patience, kid.

(*And I realize that it takes a lot of patience to accomplish the things Dad has accomplished in his life - climbing mountains, painting watercolors, making maps - all of these things take patience - they are neither quick nor easy.*)

I tell Dad that I went over to the neighbor's house and thanked him for helping pick him up and put him back in the car. I tell Dad the neighbor was surprised to learn that he is 99 - the neighbor mentioned how strong Dad's arms were, and how fit he is. Dad starts laughing.

Dad: Did you tell him I pole-vaulted 13 feet at the UW, back when there were just bamboo poles?

Karen: No, but I'll be sure to do that. (*Watching Dad paint.*) Are you planning to add some green to those trees? They look kind of blue.

Dad: Yeah, or I'll just get rid of them. (*By the time he's done for the day, Dad's magically turned the blue trees into blue ridges in the background.*)

Eventually it's time to pack up and get Dad back home. We walk out to the car - he remembers that this is the concrete he fell on yesterday, and makes sure to not do that today.

Dad: (*In the car on the way home.*) I love you, Karen.

Karen: I love you, too, Dad. (*We squeeze each other's hands.*)

Dad: I love everyone in my family. I'm happy about the way my family has turned out. We all love each other.

Karen: Yes, we do.

I get Dad back to his home and unload him. We get him sitting on his bed. He looks ready for a nap.

Dad: Are you going to take me to that thing in LA tonight?

Karen: There's nothing in LA tonight.

Dad: I don't need to go to LA?

Karen: Nope. You're right where you need to be right now.

Dad: Oh. (*He thinks about this.*) I thought I was supposed to be in LA.

Karen: Nope. You're just tired, Dad. You're ready for a nap.

Dad: Yeah. Probably.

Karen: I love you.

Dad: I love you, too.

"I Like Watching You Paint"
July 8, 2017

When I get to Dad's home, he's sitting at the dining room table finishing breakfast. There's a *Track and Field* magazine next to his plate. He says it's a good magazine, and is happy that he's getting it at his home now - and he points to the address label which has his name on it. I look through it and see a picture of a guy hurdling. Dad says he likes the hurdles - because it combines running and jumping. I ask Dad if he's ever hurdled. He says yes, when he was in the decathlon. I blink a couple times - trying to process - and then I ask him if he did the decathlon in high school...? He says he did it at the UW. It was an informal thing for all the UW track and field people at the end of the season, he says. I ask him how he did, and he says he came in second. "The guy who got first was a pole-vaulter, also." I say I'm not surprised - pole-vaulters have to have strong arms AND strong legs.

Dad finishes his green juice and then gets up and works his way to my car for a drive.

I pull over to the Sisters Espresso, and he says, "The usual place," and smiles. He knows he's going to get a root beer float here. I get him his float and my lavender green iced tea. He thanks me, and we head to my house.

He settles in to work on his painting. "How'd all that pink get there?!" he asks, seeing the pink he put on the slopes of his mountain. And, looking at another part of his picture, "I don't like all that blue there - I'm going to have to wash that out," he says. He gets his brush wet and gets to work.

Karen: When was the first time you realized you'd painted a good picture?

Dad: When I was one years-old.

Karen: When you were one?!

Dad: One is the best time to paint because you have confidence. You know you're doing the best you can do.

(*I think about this and it makes a kind of sense to me. I find a picture of Dad's grandson, Xander, painting when he was just a toddler and show it to Dad.*)

Karen: Here's Xander painting when he was little.

Dad: Does he still paint?

(*I bring up another picture of Xander painting as a young man.*)

Dad: Do you have some more work of his I can see?

(*I go to Xander's Amazon page and show Dad the covers of Xander's books - which Xander created from his own paintings.*)

Dad: These are really good. Was he inspired by me? (*Dad's smiling when he asks this.*)

Karen: Yes, he was. (*I'm remembering the time Xander hopped in the car with me and we drove down to his Grandpa and Grandma's a couple years ago - not long before they moved out of their old house. I remember Xander and I watching Dad paint at his table.*)

Dad: Do you paint?

Karen: Yes, but I'm not particularly good at it.

(*And it suddenly occurs to me that Dad might like it if I painted while he painted. So I get out another pad of watercolor paper and start painting next to him. I'm feeling self-conscious, though, because I am painting next to a professional. I expect to hear some criticism.*)

Dad: I like watching you paint.

Karen: You do?!

Dad: Yes.

(*I'm feeling all teary now. I realize I've never painted with Dad before.*)

Soon Dad is falling asleep. I ask him if he needs a nap, and he says he's always ready for a nap these days.

Dad: I sleep most of the time now. I'm preparing to pass.

Karen: You're preparing to pass?

Dad: Yes. (*Pause.*) I'm tired all the time now.

We load Dad back into the car. It's time to take him back to his home so he can lie down in his own bed and sleep.

Dad: How's Mom doing?

Karen: (*For whatever reason, I find myself jumping in with the truth this time.*) Mom passed, Daddy.

Dad: Mom passed? When did she pass?

Karen: She passed five months ago. (*He asks about the memorial service and I talk to him about that.*)

(*We pass a cemetery.*)

Dad: (*Points to the cemetery.*) I don't want to be buried in the ground when I die.

Karen: We're going to put Mom's ashes on Rainier this summer. Would you like us to put your ashes with Mom's when you pass on?

Dad: Yes. Above Alta Vista, over-looking the Nisqually Glacier.

Karen: That's what we'll do then.

Dad: I'm all alone now.

Karen: No, Dad. I'm right here.

We get back to his home and Dad asks how we chose this place for him. I tell him that Dave and I looked around and found this place and it felt like the right place for him. "These are good people," I tell Dad. And he nods his head.

Dad makes his way back to his bedroom and sits on the bed. Gwen and Melissa come in to see how he's doing.

Dad: (*Humbly.*) Thanks for taking me in.

(*Gwen and Melissa let him know that they're glad he's with them.*)

Dad: I'm going to lie down and sleep now.

Karen: I love you, Dad.

Dad: I love you, too.

"I'd Rather Go for a Drive"
July 11, 2017

Dad is still in bed when I get to his place this morning. Gwen tells me he'd had a rough day the day before - woke up from a nightmare believing he'd been kidnapped. But today when I walk into his room he pats the bed next to him and asks me to sit down, and he seems coherent and himself. He grabs my hand and squeezes it.

I show him a letter that his niece, Debby, sent him, and read it out loud to him as he follows along. He says, "Debby always worked so hard. She had three jobs at one time. I'm glad she's been able to finally retire." Debby included pictures of her grandsons - one of them has "Dee" as a middle name. I told Dad that Debby's grandson got his middle name from him. Dad says, "Oh! He's named after me?!" He's really touched by this. "I always really liked Debby. She's a nice person," he says.

I ask Dad if he'd like to go for a drive today, or if he'd like to just rest. He says a drive would be nice.

It takes a while for Gwen to help him get dressed and ready to go. When Dad finally appears with his walker he suddenly stops and says he has to sit down. Right now. We position a chair for him and he collapses into it. His face has lost its color. He says he feels like he's going to throw up and Gwen fetches a bowl for him. He dry retches, and moans. I try to call his doctor's office, but am not able to get through. Gwen asks me if I would like her to call an ambulance - I look over at Dad - look back at Gwen, and say yes.

Within minutes, it seems, the paramedics have arrived. They are efficient, friendly, up-beat, competent, and they all have brilliant white smiles. They could be on the cover of some celebrity paramedic magazine. They take Dad's blood pressure, check his heart rate, listen to his lungs. They ask Dad if he'd like to go to the hospital. He says, "I'd rather go for a drive in the country with my daughter." The paramedics laugh, and agree that sounds a lot more fun. They ask Dad to stand up so they can take his standing blood pressure, and then tell him he can sit down again. Perhaps thinking this is some kind of test - one that will determine if he has to go to the hospital or not - Dad says, "I don't need to sit down. I'm fine standing." But we assure him it's okay for him to sit, and he finally sits back down. One of the paramedics tells us it's up to us what we want to do - Dad's blood pressure is low, but not so low that it's scary - still, they can take him to the hospital if we want that - or not, if we want THAT. Dad says, "I don't want to go to the hospital." And so it's decided: Country drive.

(*As we're driving through Burlington...*)
Dad: I've had a lot of changes in my life in the last few months. (*Pause.*) So have you.
Karen: Yup. We're in this together. Drink your water. The paramedics said to drink lots of fluids so you don't have to go to the hospital.
Dad: I don't want to go to the hospital. (*Starts slurping his water through the straw.*)
(*We stop at the espresso place and I get him his root beer float and myself a lavender green iced tea. Then we drive to LaConner - I'm going to pay a bill and pick up Dad's mail from his old place.*)
Dad: This is a nice little town.
Karen: Yes, it is. You lived here with Mom for a bit.
(*We turn down the street where he lived and approach his old apartment building.*)
Karen: Do you remember this building?
Dad: Yeah, I lived here with Mom for a while, I think.
Karen: Okay, I'm going to go in and get your mail. Do NOT leave the car. I'll be right back!
Dad: Why would I leave the car? Where is there for me to go?
(*We get through with our LaConner errands and I head out towards Rexville. I stop at the Snowgoose Produce place and buy a couple strips of smoked salmon, some squeaky cheese, and some chocolate-covered hazelnuts, and we chow down on lunch. We head towards Conway.*)
Dad: There are some nice older homes out here.
Karen: Yes, there are. And I like the old barns, too.
(*Dad nods.*)

Dad: Where are we going now? I need a bed to lie down on.
Karen: I'll take you home.

We arrive back at his home and Gwen comes to help him into the house. He tells her he needs to use the bathroom. I know it's time for me to go. I kiss Dad on the cheek and tell him I love him.

"That's for Mom, Too"
July 13, 2017

I visit Dad in the early afternoon. Melissa lets me know he's having a rough day - hasn't gotten out of bed, yet, or eaten. I go in to see him. He's watching an old black and white movie on TV. He smiles when he sees me come in. I sit down next to him on the bed and he asks me if I've come to take him home. I tell him he is home, and he says, "Oh yeah! That's right. This is my room. I'm just waking up." He asks me how Mom is doing and I tell him she's doing fine. He says we need to pray for her, and I say we can do that. I tell him that David is coming up to visit in a couple days and he smiles, and says, "Good!" Then I tell him I'm going to sing a song for him - a song Mom always used to sing to me, and I sing into his ear:

> "In Thee I have no pain or sorrow,
> No anxious thought, no load of care.
> Thou art the same today, tomorrow;
> Thy love and truth are everywhere."
> (Frances A. Fox)

When I finish he nods his head and says, "That's for Mom, too." And I agree.

Dad: Am I going to go out with you now?
Karen: No, you just stay here and rest.
(*Dad nods his head.*)
Dad: I love you, Karen.
Karen: I love you, too.

"Behind Your Ears"
July 16, 2017

I spend the morning at Dad's place to finish scanning his K2 slides into the computer (David started this project yesterday). Dad is in bed when I get there, watching an old Spencer Tracy-Katharine Hepburn movie. (When I say Dad's "in bed" what that usually means is that most of his body is in bed, but his legs are dangling over the side - and his feet are moving). I lean over him to tell him I love him, and he puts his hands on my face and then gently tucks my hair behind my ears. "Behind your ears," he says. I ask him how he's feeling, and he says he's doing fine. He says, "I love you." And I tell him I love him, too.

I go out to work on his slides, and Gwen gets Dad dressed and brings him out to eat breakfast at the table next to me while I work. Dad asks me what I'm learning - and I tell him I'm learning how to use the scanner so I can scan his slides. He smiles and nods.

It takes a while to get all his slides scanned, and then Gwen sets up the room so we can have a slideshow using the original slides and Dad's old slide projector. Dad is talking about going back to bed, but I tell him we're going to show his K2 slides now - and he kind of perks up and says, "Oh. Okay." Gwen brings in the other residents and her grandson joins us.

Dad to me: You need to speak if I lose my voice. In fact... you just do all the speaking.

Karen: Okay.

Dad's slideshow always starts with a picture of a senior citizen with spunk. It brings back happy memories when I see that slide come up. Some of the slides are backwards, some are upside-down - but I tell Dad I'll take it home and fix all that for next time. He nods his head and tells me how to tell when the slides are in the slide carousel the right way. About half-way through the slideshow - after pictures of tents perched on cliffs, and steep icy slopes, and hair-raising rock climbs - there's this picture of a sandy beach and palm trees. Remembering what Dad usually says when he gets to this part of the slideshow, I say: "The climbers were all realizing at this point that they could have been spending their vacation time in a much different way." Our audience laughs. Then there are the slides that show where the accident happened - and I talk about the death of one of Dad's teammates, Art Gilkey, and the heroism of Pete Schoening, who saved Dad's life and the lives of four other climbers with his famous belay. The slideshow ends with the slides that show the climbers making their way back to civilization.

There's applause at the end of the show, and Lee, the wife of one of the residents, tells Dad how much she's enjoyed the slideshow of his K2 adventure. Dad thanks her, and they talk a bit about mountaineering.

Karen: Do you remember showing these slides to my eighth graders?

Dad: (*Nods his head.*) You've seen this show enough times that you can present it from now on for me.

Karen: Okay.

(*I wheel Dad back to his room.*)

Dad: I never dreamed I'd have a daughter like you.

Karen: I'm so blessed to have you for my Dad.

Dad: I love you.

Karen: I love you, too.

"It Has Been an Interesting Day"
July 18, 2017

When I get to Dad's place he's finishing breakfast. I tell him he has a doctor's appointment, and we're leaving in ten minutes and he nods his head. No time to use the bathroom, I tell him, and he nods his head again.

Dad: I like taking drives with you.

Karen: I like taking drives with YOU.

Dad: What's on the schedule today?

Karen: Well, first you have a doctor's appointment, and then after that we'll take a drive through the country and I'll buy you a root beer float.

Dad: Sounds like a good day.

For some reason, all the coins I usually keep in one of my cup holders are all over the floor on the passenger side of my car. Dad asks, "Do you have to keep money on the floor to get customers in here?"

We get to the doctor's office. Dad's weighed, has his blood pressure taken and heart rate checked.

The doctor checks his puffed-up leg and the red mark on it. She thinks it could be a blood clot. She wants Dad taken to the hospital for an ultrasound. She leaves to arrange this.

Once she leaves Dad lets me know he thinks this is all a rip-off. (*The bottom line is he doesn't want to go to the hospital.*) He says I sound like those old ladies in the nursing home who want to take him to the hospital. He's not a happy camper. The nurse comes in and gives me directions to the ultrasound place - she draws a map. I know the place she's talking about right away.

By this time Dad's window of time is running out before he's going to need to use the bathroom - and once he gets in the bathroom he usually stays for an hour or so. The ultrasound is scheduled for 2:30 the nurse tells me. It is 12:30 now.

Dad: Where are we going now?

Karen: I'm going to buy you a root beer float.
Dad: That sounds good.

I buy Dad his float and take him back to his place to use the bathroom for an hour. I go to Fred Meyer's for a sandwich. I pick Dad up at 2:00 and we head for the ultrasound place. I find a parking spot near the ultrasound place and help Dad get out of the car. When we get into the hospital I spy a wheelchair, and Dad asks if he can use it. I stow his walker behind a door and help him get in the wheelchair. We roll into the ultrasound place. Wait in line a bit. Then we're told that, although I am at the place the nurse drew on the map, I am in the wrong place, and at the wrong time. The appointment's actually at 2:50 at an ultrasound place a couple blocks away. But I can wheel Dad through this hospital, and then roll him through another building and end up where we're supposed to be. A volunteer says she can show me. So she leads me through this maze, up an elevator three floors, and into a corner of another building where everyone is cheerful and fun and there are smiling children. We wait.

There's a photo of mountains on the wall. I point to it. Dad says he doesn't recognize the mountains - and then a moment later he says, "The Selkirks. British Columbia." I tell him he's amazing, and he says, "I know."

Soon Howard, the ultrasound technician, comes out to fetch Dad.

After the ultrasound, I wheel Dad around the buildings, down the street, and to where I parked my car. I help him get in, and then wheel the wheelchair back where I found it, and grab Dad's walker.

When we get back to Dad's place he looks me directly in the eyes and says, "I love you for doing all this for me. Thank you."

I tell him I love to do this for him.

We get him back into the house and he goes to his bed.

Dad: It has been an interesting day.
Karen: (*Laughing.*) Yes, it has, Daddy. I love you.
Dad: I love you, too, Karen.

Test Subject
July 19th, 2017

Yesterday the ultrasound determined that Dad has a mega blood clot in his leg. Today I need to get him into the lab for a blood test. When I arrive at Dad's place he is finishing breakfast. He's happy to see me, but he has a look of concern on his face, too. He says something about research and tests. I don't really understand what he's talking about, but I figure it'll sort itself out eventually, and we get him loaded up in my car.

As we're driving to the lab, Dad says, "I want to know why I was chosen to be the subject of these tests. I want to see the documents."

I realize, then, that Dad doesn't understand why he's going to the lab. It's hard to explain to him as I'm driving along, but when I park in front of the lab I get out a piece of paper and write: "You have a blood clot in your leg. You're getting a blood test so the doctor can figure out what kind of medicine to give you, and how much."

Dad reads the note and asks, "Why didn't my doctor tell me this?" I don't know how to answer that - I know the doctor was talking about all of this in front of Dad and probably thought he'd understood what was going on, but Dad is profoundly deaf and it's obvious he didn't hear her when she was discussing his situation. Now that Dad understands why he's been driven to the lab, he's ready to do what he needs to do there. But when we get to the door of the lab we see a sign that says it's closed. Permanently. It has been closed since November, actually. The sign lists two other labs, though, that we might go to. Dad, reading the sign, understands that this lab isn't going to work for us, so we head back to the car, load back up, and set out for the lab in Sedro-Woolley.

When we get there a nice young woman sees Dad getting out of the car and sees his walker - and says, "Here. Let me hold the door for you." And she stands there, smiling a friendly smile, while Dad makes his way to the door. When Dad gets up to her, he looks at her and smiles and thanks her. (*Dad always makes a point of*

*thanking people for helping him - he says it doesn't cost anything to
be polite to people, so why shouldn't he?*)

We get inside the lab, wait a short time, and then the receptionist dons a lab coat and turns into a phlebotomist - sort of like Clark Kent becoming Superman. She is very cool, and very efficient. Dad watches her stick the needle in his arm - and does not flinch even the teensiest bit. They are a good team and in short order are done with the blood work.

We head back out to the car - a nice man holding the door open for Dad - and Dad again thanking the door-opener.

Dad: I could use a root beer float.

Karen: (*Heading to the nearest root beer float place.*) You have earned one.

"Are You Going for a Drive?"
July 23, 2017

Dad is still in bed, watching an old movie, when I get to his place about noon. I lean over to show him my face and say hi. He smiles and says, "I love you, Karen." I tell him I love him, too. I ask him if he wants to get up and he asks, "What for?" I say that if he just wants to stay in bed and rest that's fine - but even as I'm speaking I can tell the wheels are turning in his head, and he asks, "Are you going for a drive?" I tell him we could go for a drive if he wants, and he says he'll get up.

When I start out on our drive Dad wonders why I'm heading west, rather than east towards the mountains. I tell him I'd like to head towards the water today. He thinks about this and says graciously, "You go wherever you want to go." (*I think he might have realized at this point that we are nearing the place where I get him his root beer float.*)

We stop for the root beer float and my lavender green iced tea and then continue west. After a bit, Dad turns to me and says, "Thank you." (*There's something very sweet about the way he always thanks me for even the littlest things. It's never said off-handedly. It's always said in the way a little child might say it for something genuinely appreciated.*)

I stop by the house - Scott is painting the side of it - he stops and comes down off the ladder to say hi to Dad. Dad and Scott shake hands and talk for a moment about the work Scott is doing on the house. Then Dad and I continue on our adventure.

As we drive towards Bayview State Park, Dad says, "Scotty is a hard-working man." I agree that, yes, he is.

We drive to the park and then turn around in the parking lot and head back to Dad's place - driving past green fields and potato blossoms and farm houses. As we're driving by the field near where we used to live 30 years ago, Dad says: "That's the field where you found Christmas dog, isn't it?" I tell him it is. "She'd been shot in the head when you found her," he remembers. "You brought her home." Then he asks me if she's gone now, and I tell him she is. "Did she die of old age?" he asks. I tell him yes, she was 12 when she passed. Dad says, "She was a really special dog." And I agree with him. It really touches me that he remembers our Christmas dog.

Dad asks where we're going now, and I tell him I'm taking him home. I'm not sure he'll recognize his home when he sees it, but, when we get to his place, he accepts that this is his home, and says, "My home away from home. One of them."

Gwen comes out to help Dad get in the house. When he gets to the top of the stairs, and onto the main floor, I turn to him to say good-bye and to tell him I love him. He says, "I love you, too, Karen."

"How Much Can We Get for It?"
July 24, 2017

Dad's still in bed when I get there at 2:00. Gwen gets him groomed and dressed and he sits down at the dining room table with me. He's, understandably, confused about where he lives now (he's experienced a lot of changes in the last couple years), but I explain it all to him - show him the notes I'd written to him before. He remembers, then, that Moz is gone. "She was the best companion," he says, tearing up. "We could talk about anything." I show him the pictures from her memorial service and he sees himself surrounded by his friends and family.

He looks up at Gwen - trying to sort out the last five months of his life - "Do I live in your home now?" he asks her. I tell him that Gwen's home is his home. He pauses a moment - thinking about this, and then asks, "How much can we get for it?" Gwen and I both start cracking up.

After a while I ask Dad what he'd like to do now. He says he wants to go for a drive, so we put his shoes on his feet, and his faithful old alpine hat on his head, and load him up in the car.

We stop for his root beer float at Sisters Espresso. He - as always - thanks me for his treat. We drive to my house - I show Dad all the painting Scotty is doing - and Scott comes around the house just then, sees us in the car, and comes to give Dad a handshake and a hug through the window. Then Dad and I continue on our adventure up Bow Hill Road and to I-5.

Dad wants to know if Mom said any last words, if she'd been in pain, if she'd known she was dying. I tell him she hadn't been in any pain - she'd died peacefully in her sleep while I slept on the couch next to her. Dad nods, comforted that she hadn't been in pain. I tell him she'd known she was passing, and tell him her last word to me had been, "Okay." I tell him she said she loved all of us - and that she had loved him very much. Dad nods, taking it in.

When I bring Dad back to his home I show him the poetry book I gave him, and show him the poems I'd written about Mom's last day with me. I tell him I'll leave the book on the bed for him for when he's ready to read it.

Karen: I love you, Daddy.
Dad: I love you, too, Karen.

Today Was the Day
July 26, 2017

For a while now Gwen has mentioned that she'd like to take Dad and another resident, Joe, up to the Shadow of the Sentinels Trail on the Mount Baker Highway - it's a nice wheel-chair accessible trail through an old growth forest, and there are views of Mount Baker nearby.

And this is the day!

I get to the home as Dad is finishing up breakfast. He knows we are going somewhere today - he thinks we're going to the ocean - but I let him know we're going to the mountains today. I tell him we're going on an adventure. Melissa tells Dad we need to prepare him for our adventure, and Dad says: "You don't prepare for an adventure."

Dad says he can't drive anymore. He says, "I don't have a license for the car or for me. I need to take it easy from here on."

We load Dad and Joe up in Gwen's car. As soon as we get packed in there, Dad says he needs his accordion. I go inside and grab his harmonica and come back outside with it - Dad sees it and his eyes light up - he thanks me for hearing him. As we set out, he asks if I've brought his jacket, ice axe, and sleeping bag - and I explain that this is a short trail and we'll be home by the end of the afternoon. He says, "It's nice to not have to be the one in charge."

When we get to the trail, he perks up. He asks if we're getting out here, and I say yes. Gwen and I load Joe and Dad up in the wheelchairs and set out down the boardwalk into the forest. It's beautiful and quiet in there. Butterflies flit among the devil's club; huckleberries and blueberries grow from the bushes; moss hangs from the branches like green lace; and we can hear an owl hooting from somewhere off the trail.

Dad thanks me for bringing him into the mountains. I tell him this was Gwen's idea and he nods, filing that away. He says, "I love you for doing this with me." I ask him if he's enjoying this walk, and he nods and says yes, he is. He says: "I'm going to write a letter to the superintendent of the park and thank him for making this walk accessible to the old." And it occurs to me that a letter from Dee

Molenaar, thanking the park service for building this trail, might be a pretty awesome letter for a park service superintendent to get.

I want Dad to see the treetops above him, but he says it hurts his neck to crane his head back. Gwen says she can help him - and she gets behind his wheelchair and tilts it back, and tells Dad to look at the canopy above him. For the first time Dad really opens his eyes to what's going on up there. He says, "Oh!" Then he tells me to take pictures of the treetops. I tell him I already have. He asks me if I used a wide angle lens - and I assure him I did. "Good," he says, nodding his head.

We load Joe and Dad back into the car after our walk and head for a bridge that has a really nice view of Mount Baker. We stop on the bridge so Dad can take in the sight of Baker - big and beautiful and smack dab in front of his eyes. He asks to make sure I'm taking pictures of the mountain - and I tell him I am.

Then we head down the mountain for lunch at Annie's Pizza Restaurant in Concrete.

Sitting in Annie's Pizza Restaurant after our walk reminds me of other times when I've sat in restaurants with Dad after hikes and climbs - there's that same cozy, sun-toasted, happily tired feeling. Dad turns his chair so he can observe the other patrons in the restaurant, drinks his root beer float, and makes himself comfortable. "This is nice," he says. My thoughts, exactly.

As we head back to his home, Dad turns to Gwen and thanks her for this nice day. Gwen grins and agrees it was a nice day.

We unload Joe and Dad and help them into the house.

Karen: I love you, Daddy.

Dad: I love you, too.

My Daddy Is a Hero
July 29, 2017

My daddy is a hero. I found a letter from one of Dad and Mom's old friends among Mom's stuff and wrote the friend back, updating her on Mom's passing and Dad's circumstances. Mom and Dad's friend sent me a letter in return. Here's part of what she shared: "Your dad has been a dear friend both to me and my late husband, Don - Dee guided Don to the top of Mt. Rainier, and the two shared many other adventures through the years. Did you know Dee saved Don's life one time when the two had taken a group of young boys on an overnight hike? The weather turned bad on them and they needed to set up tents before all were soaked. Don and Dee managed to get tents up, but were very wet and cold in the doing, and Don slipped into hypothermia. Dee recognized that, and was able to strip Don and provide his own body heat, thus saving him from a sad end!"

I've heard several stories like this from people in the last several months - stories where Dad's quick reactions saved people from sliding into crevasses and so forth. Dad has never shared these stories with me himself. He's never tooted his own horn.

I get a flashback now of the time Dad saved me from sliding into a crevasse when we were coming down from the summit of Rainier. Dad handled it so quickly and quietly and matter-of-factly - a quick belay - that I never thought much of it at the time. Now I do, though. I never remember being scared when I climbed with Dad. I always knew he would take care of me.

"That Looks Like My First Car"
August 1, 2017

Karen: Do you just want to stay in bed and rest today?

Dad: (*Looking up at me, hopefully.*) Unless somebody wants to go for a drive.

Karen: Do you want to go for a drive?

Dad: Yeah.

A half an hour later Gwen has Dad dressed and fed, and we load him into my car. I head south on I-5.

Dad: When you and Scott retire are you going to travel the world?

Karen: That sounds fun!

Dad: I've seen a lot of the world. (*This is an understatement.*) I can tell you where NOT to go.

Karen: Where should we not go?

Dad: New York City.

(*I've been to New York City and enjoyed it - but I'm wondering when Dad went and what he experienced there.*)

Karen: Where else should we not go?

Dad: Well, you're on the freeway. Any place from the freeway is fine. It's easy to go anywhere from here. (*Dad's looking at the scenery as I drive.*) Where are you taking me?

Karen: I thought we'd go south and see if we can see Rainier. It might be kind of hazy today, though. There's a forest fire in Canada.

Dad: Rainier's too far. Baker will be all clouded in today. (*We pass a sign for LaConner.*) Let's go to the old waterfront part of LaConner.

Karen: You want to go to LaConner?

Dad: Yeah.

(*As we're driving through the countryside towards LaConner, Dad is taking note of what he sees.*)

Dad: This area looks a lot like the midwest, except for the hills in the background.

(*We pass a sign with a Dutch name on it and I point to it.*)

Dad: Roozengarde - there's a Dutch name. We could be driving through the Netherlands - except for the mountains in the background.

We get to LaConner and Dad decides he wants to go to a museum. I've wanted to take Dad to the Skagit Historical Museum since he moved up here a year ago. Maybe today is the day this will happen. I drive to the museum and park maybe 30 yards from it. I don't realize there are a lot of parking spaces closer to the museum, but, when I park where I park, 30 yards doesn't seem like much of a walk. I am wrong. We unload Dad and his walker, and begin the walk to the museum. After about ten yards Dad says he needs to sit down, and we find a place for him to sit on a little wall.

Karen: Let me go see if they have wheelchairs in there. Stay here. Are you alright?

Dad: (*Nodding.*) Okay.

I go into the museum to see if they have wheelchairs. They don't. A rolling chair seems promising, though. I ask if I can use it to get Dad around, and Ann, the woman tending the counter, says sure. I bring the chair down to where Dad is sitting, and help Dad get into the rolling chair. A nice couple about to go into the museum approaches us to help. Steve says he can push Dad from the back, and Danielle guards Dad from the side, and I pick up Dad's feet so they don't drag on the concrete. When we get Dad inside he decides he wants to use his walker in there. He heads into the room that displays a history of technology.

Dad: That looks just like my first car!

Karen: Your first car was a Model-T Ford?

Dad: Yeah. Model-T Ford. 1925.

I am grinning now. I love that I'm walking through an historical museum with a walking piece of history. Dad is starting to get tired again, and we bring back the rolling chair for him to sit in. We head into the World War II exhibit. Dad served in the Coast Guard in World War II and he seems fascinated by what he sees here. He notes that the Coast Guard doesn't seem to be represented, but says that's okay - the Coast Guard was more in the South Pacific, and this exhibit is more about the campaign in Europe.

Danielle, the woman who helped Dad earlier, approaches Dad to tell him she looked him up in *Wikipedia* and wants to thank him for his service during the war. Dad thanks her and asks her if she was in the Coast Guard. Danielle says no, but her brother was. Dad likes that. I get a picture of Dad with Steve and Danielle. Dad asks me their names, and I introduce them. He shakes their hands. He has just met two new friends.

Dad is tired now. He's ready to go home. With colossal effort he manages to use his walker to get himself back to the car - which I have now parked right next to the door. He asks where we're going next, and I tell him I'm going to get him a root beer float and then take him home. He nods his head in agreement. I stop for his root beer float.

Karen: You really earned this one.

(*Dad nods his head in complete agreement, and then we head to his home. Dad looks completely exhausted. He has sucked down his root beer float by the time we get to his place. I open the passenger door for him, and inch by inch he turns himself around in his seat.*)

Dad: Every little movement takes so much energy now. And I need to rest after every movement. (*He closes his eyes and sighs and leans back to rest for a few moments, before making another movement to get out of the car.*) You have a doddering old Dad.

Karen: No. I have a mountain-climbing Dad.

Dad: That was a long time ago. (*He looks up at the house.*) I think I'm going to take a little nap when I get in there.

Karen: I love you, Daddy. I'm proud to be your daughter.

Dad: I love you, too, and I'm proud to have you for a daughter.

"I Look Good in Every Shirt"
August 3, 2017

Karen: You have an eye doctor's appointment today.
Dad: I do? When?
Karen: We're going to leave in five minutes.
Dad: Okay. (*Starts digging into his cereal.*)
Karen: You look good in that shirt.
Dad: I look good in every shirt.
Dad: I love you.
Karen: I love you, too.

Soon we're at the doctor's office. Almost as soon as we arrive Dad and I are ushered back into the examination room.
Doctor's assistant: How many fingers do you see?
Dad: Three. But I'm guessing.
Doctor's assistant: Good guess! It's three.
(*While the doctor is getting his doctor-machine ready, Dad and I quietly wink back and forth at each other.*)

The doctor leaves for a bit. Dad asks me what I'm thinking about. I tell him I've been studying Spanish on the internet and I'm thinking about Spanish words. He nods and asks me if I'm getting paid to learn Spanish. I tell him no, I'm doing it for fun. I tell him I'm going to learn Dutch next. I ask him if he knows any Dutch words, and he grins and says, "Godverdomme." He says he used that phrase a lot when he was milking cows and would get hit in the face by a tail.

The appointment done, I stop at the desk to make Dad's next appointment, and Dad heads down the hall and towards the door. He is going at a good clip.
Karen: And he's gone. (*The receptionist starts laughing.*) I guess I'll call you to make an appointment later.
Receptionist: That'll work.

On the way back to Dad's place...

Karen: Did Pop have a sense of humor?

Dad: He taught my brother and me how to fart at the table. And then Mom would say, "Oh, Pete!"

Dad: I haven't seen Mom in a while. (*Pause.*) Is she gone?

Karen: Yes, she is. She's been gone five months now.

Dad: Was there a memorial service for her?

Karen: Yes. You were there.

Dad: I was there? (*He thinks about this for a moment.*) Did anyone recognize that I'm not my old self?

Karen: Everyone knew you were you.

Dad: Was I friendly? Did I put on a good front?

Karen: You were great!

"They've Taken Me a Lot of Places"
August 10, 2017

Dad's finishing up his brunch when I get there. He doesn't see me at first and then he turns his head and his eyes light up and he says, "Karen!" I ask him if he'd like to go for a drive today and he says, "I wouldn't mind."

As we're helping him get up Melissa tells him he has good legs. Dad says, "I know. They've taken me a lot of places." Melissa tells him how lucky he is to be going for a drive and Dad says, "I really am."

We head out of town. Dad notes that the air is smoky, and I tell him the smoke is coming from Canadian wildfires. He thinks about this and then observes, "Pieces of Canada are landing in the United States." And I guess this is true - although I haven't thought about it that way until he says it.

We stop for our usual: Root beer float for Dad; iced lavender green iced tea for me. And then we head west. When we get to the end of the road, I ask him which direction he wants to go and he points right. Eventually he directs us back to Chuckanut.

Karen: Where would you like to go now?

Dad: I'd like to drive by your house.

(*We go to my house, and I pull into the driveway.*)

Karen: Do you want to get out here and go inside?

Dad: (*Thinking about this.*) No. I'm good. I'd need to walk to get in the house.

Karen: Yes, you would.

Dad: I'm fine staying in the car. (*He's grinning at himself.*)

Karen: (*Grinning back at Dad.*) Okay. We'll just stay in the car today.

I head back towards Dad's home. As we get closer to his house he asks where else we could go, and I realize he's not ready to go back home, yet. And I realize I'm not ready to take him home, yet. So I head towards Sedro-Woolley. At some point Dad closes his eyes and nods off. He's sleeping and quiet, but I can feel the presence of his life next to me, and I'm suddenly just so glad he's still with me - even if he's just sleeping. I store away this moment in my memory.

I drive around for another half hour maybe. As we're nearing his home he wakes up and sees where he is. I pull into his driveway. He wonders what's next on the agenda - and I tell him I think there's a track meet on television. He perks up at this news. "Oh good!" he says. Melissa comes out and helps me get him out of the car and heading towards his room. The track meet is on his television and he gets himself comfortable to watch it.

Karen: I love you, Daddy.

Dad: I love you, too, Karen.

"I've Been There, You Know"
August 13, 2017

When I get to Dad's place he's just finished watching a show on Machu Picchu on the Science channel. He points to the screen and says, "I was just watching a show on Machu Picchu. I've been there, you know." (I nod my head - there are very few places Dad hasn't been.) "Have you ever been there?" he asks. I shake my head no.

The TV screen is asking us if we want to watch the next show - this one is on the terracotta warriors in China. I click the button and the show starts.

Dad: Oh. This is going to be interesting. I enjoy watching these shows. This one is about the soldiers in China that were all carved from one piece of sandstone.

(I know this isn't true - but Dad's idea is kind of a cool one - I figure it takes a certain amount of intelligence to come up with something like that. So I nod my head. I'm guessing once he starts watching the show he'll see that these guys weren't made from sandstone, and I see no need to correct him.)

Dad: I haven't seen Mom for a long time - a year, I think. Have you seen her?

Karen: No. (*I shake my head.*)

Dad watches the expression on my face for a moment, and then asks, "Is she not alive?"

I shake my head no.

Dad wants to make sure he's getting this right and asks again, "She's not alive?"

I say no and wait to see what's going to happen next. Dad looks back at the television. I reach for his hand and give it a squeeze, and he squeezes my hand back. He's not crying this time. I think on some level he's processed Mom's death - he doesn't seem surprised by it anymore.

Gwen comes in and relays a story about a dialogue between Scott and Dad yesterday: Scott stopped in after work to see Dad, and Dad asked him something about his newspaper job, and then Dad turned to Gwen and said, "Scott and I own a half-interest in the local newspaper, you know." Dad and Scott do not own any part of the local newspaper - but, again, this is a kind of cool story, and just using the phrase "a half-interest" is a sign of intelligence, right? I turn to look at Dad and he grins back at me. What a character. Lord, I love him.

Karen: I love you, Daddy.
Dad: I love you, Karen.

"Is Mom Gone?"
August 14, 2017

When I arrive at Dad's place this morning I find him with his old friend, Kenny Foreman, and Kenny's beautiful wife, Denise. Dad has known Ken for more than 70 years - they met in the Coast Guard during World War II. Kenny went on to become one of the most renowned track and field coaches in the USA (he was inducted into the Hall of Fame in 2009).

After I get some quick pictures I tell Dad I'll give him some time with his friends and come back later for our drive.

I call his place in the early afternoon to see if Dad is still up for a drive. Cindy tells me that Dad is sitting at the table waiting for me - he's just asked Cindy if he's still going to get a drive today. Awww....

So I skoot over there and load Dad up in the car and set out for another grand adventure.

Dad: Is Mom coming with us?

Karen: No.

Dad: (*As we're heading out of town...*) Is Mom gone?

Karen: Yes. (*I reach over and grab Daddy's hand and squeeze it.*)

Dad: (*Pause.*) Did she have any last words?

Karen: She loved you. She loved you very much.

Dad: We made such a good life together.

Karen: Yes, you did.

Dad: Our children are close.

Karen: Yes, we are.

I decide to head south this time - I want to see if I can find a place for us to get a glimpse of Rainier. I'm so excited when we finally cross over the border into Snohomish County - I don't think Dad's been out of Skagit County for, like, a year - and it feels like we've passed through some huge invisible obstacle.

By the time we get to Arlington it seems clear that it's too hazy to see Rainier today, so I turn onto the road that will take us into Arlington.

Dad perk up as soon as we turn off the freeway. He looks up and sees what's in front of us. "That's the Three Fingers," he says.

Karen: Is that one on the right Pilchuck?

Dad: Yeah, Pilchuck.

Karen: Remember when we hiked up that one?

Dad: Yeah. Nice lookout tower up there. Good view from the top.

When we arrive in Arlington I decide to turn onto Highway 9 and go back to Skagit County that way. We pass some beautiful scenery. Dad's head is shifting from right to left, taking it all in. I point out Lake McMurray and Dad says, "I use to do water rights work for the state on a lot of these roads you've been taking me on. This road is Highway 9, isn't it? It travels through the foothills of the Cascades."

Dad: Thank you for taking me on these drives.

Karen: I enjoy them.

(*We take Highway 9 all the way to Sedro-Woolley and then head back to Dad's home.*)

Dad: Thanks for the nice drive. That was a nice, long, relaxing drive.

Karen: I love taking drives with you, Daddy.

Dad: I enjoy going on them.

Karen: I love you, Daddy.

Dad: I love you, too, Karen.

Moz Brought Us All Together
August 20, 2017

Moz has brought us all together - my brothers, my sons, and I. We are on the slopes of Rainier, hiking to a place where Moz and Dad always said they wanted their ashes spread when that time came.

At home there's a photo of Moz with our son, Andrew, in a child carrier on her back. Andrew's about a year old, I think, and both he and Moz are wearing grins that stretch from ear to ear. Today Andrew carries Moz on his back. Well, her ashes, anyway.

It's good to be together again - my menfolk and me. We hike up through fields of lupine and Indian paintbrush. We can hear marmots whistling. Butterflies flit among the wildflowers. When we reach our destination, we spread Moz's ashes in a fine place behind some spruce and hemlock trees. Then we stand and gaze out over the valley - taking in deep breaths of the sagey alpine air, and remembering our beloved matriarch.

I wish Dad could have traveled up here with us today, but his health wouldn't permit it, and I'm not sure he realizes she's gone.

"People Do Everything for Me Now"
August 22, 2017

Dad: I'm going to a ball game this afternoon.
Karen: You are?
Dad: Yeah, a baseball game at the local ballpark.
Karen: (*Thinking about this.*) Okay. Would you like to go for a drive right now then?
Dad: Yeah. Where haven't we been? Let's go into the mountains.
Karen. Okay.
Dad: (*As we're driving away from his home.*) I never thought my retirement would be so luxurious. People do everything for me now. All I do is sleep and eat and watch TV.
(*I nod my head in acknowledgement.*)
Dad: How's Mom doing?
Karen: She's alright.
Dad: (*Again...*) How's Mom doing?
Karen: She passed away, Daddy.
Dad: How long ago?
Karen: Six months ago.
Dad: I never got to say good-bye to her.
Karen: You said good-bye to her in the hospital. She loved you very much.

I turn us down Hwy 9 and head towards Mount Baker - I know I'm not going to be able to get us all the way to the parking lot today, but I'll go until I find a view.
Karen: We brought Mom's ashes up to Rainier last weekend.
Dad: What? I didn't hear you.
(*I pull over to the side of the road. This is important - what I'm trying to tell Dad. I find a scrap of paper and write: We took Mom's ashes up to Alta Vista last weekend.*)
Dad: (*Reads the note.*) Oh, good. Where did you put her?
Karen: On the highest point.
Dad: Good.

We drive until I see a view of Baker poking up above the hills and a turnout spot.

Karen: Look, Daddy! There's Baker!

Dad: Oh. Yeah! (*He starts moving his finger up the mountain.*) That spot there is base camp, and then we go straight up that snowfield there to the top.

Karen: Yep.

We go as far as the Van Zandt community, and then I look at the clock and realize it's time to turn around.

Dad: Are we going back now?

Karen: Yeah. It's kind of hazy today. Maybe we'll go to the Mount Baker parking lot another time.

Dad: (*Nods his head.*) Yeah.

I stop at Dairy Queen and buy us both shakes. Dad says he wants to pay this time, but I tell him he can pay next time, and he nods okay.

Dad: Let's go to the campground and eat these in the shade.

Karen: Okay. (*I don't know what campground Dad means, but I head for Sedro-Woolley's Riverfront Park, and park in the shade of some trees. We slurp our shakes and contemplate life - not talking for a while.*)

Dad: Did they have root beer floats there?

Karen: Yeah. But this is good, too, right?

Dad: Yeah.

We head back to Dad's home. When we turn onto Hwy 20, Dad knows the drive is almost done.

Dad: We're headed home now?

Karen: Yes.

Dad: Nice drive.

Karen: I enjoyed it very much.

We arrive at his home, and I go around to help Dad out of the car.

Dad: This old man really appreciates these drives.

Karen: I really enjoy them!

(Cindy and I help Dad negotiate the steps.)
Karen: I love you, Daddy.
Dad: I love you, too, Karen.

"Daddy, Mom's Gone"
August 24, 2017

I stop by to see Dad today. He's sitting in his recliner in the living room, watching a movie. "I'm watching a movie about the Titanic," he says. "It's really good. I think I've seen this one before. But it's really good."

I look at the screen and see that he's watching *Titanic* with Kate Winslet. Titanic is not one of my favorite movies, but I have to admit it was well done. "That is a good one," I agree.

"Have you seen Mom?" Dad asks. I shake my head no. He says, "I haven't seen her for a long time. We're on different schedules. We keep missing each other."

And I have to make that decision again. Do I tell him or do I not? This time it feels like I should tell him. "Daddy, Mom's gone," I say. "You said good-bye to her in the hospital. She loved you very much."

He sees the look on my face and starts to tear up. And then he does the sweetest thing. He reaches up and gently brushes the bangs back from my forehead - he does this several times. And I close my eyes and - for a moment - I'm a little girl again, with my Daddy comforting me.

"Making Busy"
August 26, 2017

Dad: I'm editing reports in preparation for publication. Tonight I leave for Washington, DC, for a conference. I'll come back in a week. When I return I'll be back in the office, making busy. Do you ever make busy?

Karen: Is that when you pretend you're busy?

Dad: (*Grinning.*) Yes. We can't bring books to work. So I need to make busy. But I enjoy my work. I'm at an age where I don't have to work. I can just work for the fun of it. Do you enjoy your work?

Karen: Yes, I do.

Dad: Good.

Karen: Next week you have some friends visiting. Your old colleague, Rick, is going to visit. And then Bob Ader's coming out to visit you and climb Glacier Peak.

Dad: (*Smiling.*) Oh, those are some of my favorite people.

"I Like That Breeze"
September 2, 2017

Karen: How are you feeling? Are you comfortable just staying in bed today?

Dad: Yeah. I could just lie here. (*Pause.*) And die here.

Karen: Or we could go for a drive.

Dad: Yeah. Let me get up and get dressed and we can go for a drive.

In the car, heading for Bow...

Dad: How has your day been?

Karen: I went for a nice bike ride this morning.

Dad: In the flats?

Karen: Yeah.

Dad: I always like bike riding. But not up the hills. (*Pause.*) Have you had lunch, yet?

Karen: Should we get you some lunch?

Dad: Yeah. Any place would be good.

(*I stop at the Sisters Espresso and get Dad his root beer float and a breakfast sandwich, and myself a lavender green iced tea.*)

Karen: I'll show you the route I took this morning on my bike ride. (*I click the odometer on my car's dashboard so I can see how far I went this morning as I retrace my route.*)

Dad: Okay.

Karen: I went down this road here...

Dad: (*Looking around.*) I've biked down here before.

(*He did. In his seventies and eighties, when he was visiting us, Dad used to borrow a bike and ride over hill and dale all over this area.*)

Dad: I wonder what the percentage of minerals is in this soil. (*Thinking.*)I wonder how much of Mount Baker is in this silt. (*Thinking.*) I wonder how many people living here know about the geology of this area.

Karen: This is an interesting question.

Dad: Have you seen any activity on Baker lately?

Karen: No. (*His question makes me a little nervous, and I glance at Baker half-expecting to see steam coming out of its crater.*)

Dad: Did you climb Baker?

Karen: Yes. With you.

Dad: (*Nods his head, remembering.*) And Scott.

Karen: Yes.

(*I retrace my route, driving down Allen, driving up Farm to Market, driving through Edison, driving down Chuckanut, down Thomas, back to Allen and to the Sisters Espresso. I figure I rode my bike about 16 and a half miles this morning.*)

Dad: Maybe we could go up to Baker today.

Karen: I don't think there's enough time today.

Dad: No. We probably couldn't climb it today.

Karen: (*I realize Dad meant CLIMBING Baker, rather than just driving up to the parking lot - and it occurs to me that, rather than being a sign of dementia, his idea to just spontaneously climb Baker is more an indication of the kind of life he led when he was younger. This is the kind of thing he probably DID do.*) No. Not enough time today.

I'm not ready to take Dad home, yet. So I turn onto Cook, and head for Bayview State Park.

Dad: (*Looking up the long hill on Josh Wilson Road.*) I remember coasting down this hill on a bike.

I drive to Bayview State Park and park facing the bay.

Dad: Shall we get out and walk on the beach?

Karen: We could walk to that bench there and look out at the water.

Dad: Okay.

(*It takes some effort and maneuvering, but we finally manage to settle ourselves on the bench. We look out at the water - there's a mom skimming her toddler's toes in the surf, and then the baby is in the water, grinning and splashing around. There're a couple of men and a daughter playing around on the beach to the right. Butterflies flutter around in the beach grass in front of our bench. The water is blue and peaceful, and a gentle breeze blows across us.*)

Dad: I like that breeze. Keeps the flies away.

Karen: Yeah. This is great. (*Noticing that Dad's eyes are sort of squinted up.*) Here, wear my sunglasses. (*I put them on Dad's head.*)

Dad: Oh. (*Smiling.*) Yeah.

Dad: I like the air. (*He watches the little girl holding her Daddy's hand as they walk back up the beach towards us. He approves.*) They're teaching her an appreciation of the beach.

Karen: (*I realize that this is what Dad did for me, too - he consciously taught me an appreciation of Nature.*) Yes.

(*For a while we sit together in companionable silence. My eyes are closed, and I'm guessing Dad's are, too. In this moment I have everything I need - I'm warm and fed and sheltered, there's fresh air to breath, and I have my daddy alive and breathing beside me.*)

Karen: Are you enjoying this?

Dad: I really am.

Eventually, it's time to go back. We make our way back to the car, and start the drive back to Dad's home.

Dad: I really enjoy these drives with you.

Karen: I do, too, Daddy.

Cindy comes out and helps me get Dad out of the car and back up the stairs into his home.

Dad: (*Heading for the recliner in the living room.*) And now it's time for a nap.

Karen: I love you, Daddy.

Dad: I love you, too.

A Whole Lot of Magic
September 4, 2017

I stop by to see Dad. He's sleeping. His brow is furrowed and he looks concerned. I put my hand in his and he squeezes it. Then I gently try to wipe the frown from his brow. He opens his eyes and sees me and his whole face lights up. "Karen!" he says, and then pulls me in for a hug, "I love you so much!"

Sometimes there's a whole lot of magic packed into just a few moments.

The Man Who Wanted Dad's Hat
September 7th, 2017

FB Friend: Would this weekend be a good time to come visit with Dee? My dream trip would include going on one of your drives with him, if that works for you. I have an old alpenstock that I would love for him to sign. (He has previously signed a couple of other ice axes for me.) I believe I have the largest collection of signed ice axes in the world. (Around 60 axes signed by around 330 different climbers, climbing authors, polar adventurers, etc.) Also, if you have any climbing memorabilia that you may be willing to part with, I may be interested in adding it to my collection.

Hope to hear back from you soon, so I can finalize my travel plans.

Thanks so much,
FB Friend

Karen: Dad would love to see you, I'm sure - and he'll sign whatever you give him to sign. I'm really stretched right now - school started this week - today was the first day with the students - I've been trying to visit with Dad, and also keep connected to my sons, husband, friends - there's a block party this weekend and it's my birthday - but, honestly, I'm not sure any other weekend is any better for me right now. There's just a lot going on here. But you don't need me with you when you visit Dad - just be prepared to talk really loud and maybe bring a pad of paper and a pen. I stopped by to see him this afternoon after school - he was struggling - he said he was trying to follow up on some leads to find out where Mom is - he said he hadn't seen her for a year - it was difficult - I didn't want him to think Mom abandoned him - so I had to tell him again that she loved him very much, that she passed on six months ago, that he was able to say good-bye to her and she was able to say good-bye to him - that her love is always with him. But... these visits take a lot out of me.

He seems to do alright with old mountain friends, though. He can spend time in that world - and I think that's good for him.

If you plan to visit this weekend, call his adult family home and let them know, and they'll have him ready for you.
You totally have to have him sign your axe.

(After this conversation, when FB Friend visited Dad, he wondered if he could take Dad's alpine hat with him as a piece of memorabilia. My brother, who had happened to stop by to visit with Dad, told him no, the hat is a family heirloom. And... yeah.)

"I'm All Mixed-up These Days"
September 11, 2017

Dad is sitting at the dining room table when I arrive there after school. I ask him if he will sign the painting for Naomi - a woman he used to know at his old place who'd been given an unsigned painting of his. He happily signs it. Then he says he'd heard it was my birthday - I tell him I already had it - and he asks me if I'll forgive him for forgetting it. I start laughing, and tell him there's nothing to forgive. He says he's all mixed-up these days. I tell him we're ALL mixed-up. He asks me if I teach my students to be mixed-up - and I tell him, no, I manage to not be so mixed-up at school.

Dad: How's Mom?
Karen: She's fine.
Dad: (*Starts tearing up even as he's asking the question.*) Is Mom gone?
Karen: Yes. (*I reach over to hold his hand.*)
Dad: I miss her.
Karen: I know, Dad. I miss her, too. But she still loves you - her love is still with us. I feel her all the time.
Dad: (*Nodding his head and sniffling.*) Where are you going now?
Karen: I'm going to LaConner to take this painting to Naomi.
Dad: Can I go with you?
Karen: Sure!

In the car...
Dad: How are the boys taking Mom's death?
Karen: We're all doing alright, Dad. It's hard, but we're all doing alright.
Dad: I never got to say good-bye to her.
Karen: You said good-bye to her in the hospital. And she said good-bye to you.
(*A little later.*)
Dad: I need to go door-to-door and ask people about their wells. (*Thinking about this...*) But I guess I could just send out letters

- ask them to check "yes" if they have a well, or "no" if they don't. I'm supposed to go to Bremerton tonight. Will you come with me?

Karen: You don't need to go to Bremerton. You're alright. There's nothing you need to do.

Dad: How's our friend, Jack?

Karen: Jack's alright. We saw him a few months ago.

Dad: How's Jack's mom, Carol?

Karen: Carol passed on last year, Daddy.

Dad: (*Looking around.*) I miss driving. I used to get in the car whenever I wanted and drive all over - up into the hills, wherever I wanted to go.

Karen: I know, Daddy. It's hard.

Dad: (*Looking across the flats.*) The glaciers made this. Brought in sand and gravel. Can you see Rainier?

Karen: I think it might be hard today.

Dad: Yeah. It's a little hazy.

Dad: Are we going home?

Karen: No, we're going to your old home.

Dad: (*Thinking.*) You brought us up here to be closer to you.

Karen: Yes. You remember! (*Pause.*) I need to pay a bill, too. But you don't need to get out of the car.

Dad: Good. It causes a lot of disruption for others when I try to move around.

Karen: (*Laughing.*) I sure love you, Daddy.

(*I stop off and pay my bill and then drive to Dad's old assisted living home.*)

Dad: I think I may have lived here.

Karen: Yes, you lived here with Moz for about a year.

Dad: (*Fiddling around with the window openers.*) How do I get out of the car?

Karen: Don't get out of the car...

Dad: I'm not going to get out of the car, but I want to know how to if I have to. I need an escape hatch.

Karen: Oh. Okay. (*I show him what thingy to pull to open the door and run inside to see if I can find Naomi to give her the painting - I figure if I don't find her in the lobby of dining area, I'll just leave it at the front desk - but I see her just as she's about to enter the elevator. She grins when she sees me and happily takes her painting from me. I tell her Dad is in the car and she comes out to say hi.*)

Naomi: Hi, Dee! (*Naomi reaches in to give Dad a hug.*)

Dad: (*Smiling a big smile.*) Hi.

(*Dad and Naomi talk for a while, and then she leaves to go back into the assisted living place. I get back in the car.*)

Dad: Do I know her?

Karen: Yes, she was Moz's good friend here. You all used to sit at the same table for meals.

(*Dad nods. We drive out of LaConner.*)

Dad: This is a nice little town.

Karen: Yes. You and Moz lived here for almost a year. You used to get ice cream there, and look at the art in that gallery over in that place.

As we're driving back to Dad's place, I see Rainier on the horizon. I pull over and point it out to Dad. He can't see it at first - and then finally sees it - but not well.

Dad: I used to be so proud of my eyesight.

Karen: I know. But you're doing really well, Daddy. You're 99, you know?

As we turn up the road to his home, Dad becomes alert. He points to his house, and tells me to turn there. When I pull up to the front door, he asks if I'm letting him out here. I tell him yes and go around to help him out.

Karen: I love you, Daddy.

Dad: I love you, too, Karen.

"I Have to Get up for Work"
September 16, 2017

Dad's sleeping when I get there. I gently stroke his forehead and then start to leave, but he opens his eyes. He smiles and says, "Oh! Thanks for coming all this way." I tell him I just stopped by to see him, and he didn't need to wake up. I tell him I love him. He says he loves me, too, and says, "I have to get up for work, anyway." I tell him no, he's fine. He can go back to sleep now. He says, "Thank you," and closes his eyes.

"That Would Be Better Than Staying in Bed"
September 20, 2017

I stop by to see Dad after school. He says, "My daughter!" and asks if we're going for a drive. I ask him if he wants to go for a drive. He says, "That would be better than staying here in bed."

Melissa helps me load him up in the car, and, as we're pulling out, Dad says, "Let's head towards the coast" and points west. So I head towards Edison.

Dad: Do you like taking drives with me?
Karen: Yes, I do.
Dad: (*Chuckling.*) We're two birds of a feather. (*Musing.*) People always pretend they're not proud of their farts.
(*A little later.*)
Dad: Does Scott want to live out here in the country?
Karen: Yes.
Dad: He can buy a couple acres out here and grow a garden.
Karen: Yep.
Dad: How's Mom?
Karen: She's alright.
Dad: What did you say?
Karen: Mom's alright.
Dad: Mom's gone?
(*The fact that Dad thinks he's heard me say that Moz is gone, makes me believe that he knew she was gone before he asked the question. I'm thinking he's needing me to confirm what he already knows. I nod my head yes.*)
Dad: I didn't even get to say good-bye.
(*I reach over and pat his leg to show my support.*)

Dad: I'm always happy to see you enter my room.
Karen: I'm always happy to see you, Dad.

We drive towards Bay View.
Dad: (*Recognizing where we are.*) We've been here a couple times.

(*I nod my head yes.*)

As we come down the hill from Bay View back into the valley, Dad scans the country in front of him.

Dad: The Skagit Valley. This is beautiful country.

Karen: Yes.

We pass through Edison and Dad asks if I live in this little cluster of houses. I tell him no, I live a little beyond Edison. We pass the Sisters Espresso where I usually buy him a root beer float and he points to it.

Karen: Yeah - that's our place. It's closed now.

Dad: It's closed?

Karen: Yeah.

(*Dad nods his head in acceptance.*)

As we pull into the driveway of his home, Dad asks if this is his permanent home now, and I nod my head.

Karen: I smell dinner.

Dad: Good!

(*I help Dad up the stairs. There's a place set for him at the dining room table and he heads that direction.*)

Karen: I love you, Daddy.

Dad: I love you, too.

Autumn

I've graduated from university now. Dad has led me to the summits of Rainier and Hood by this time. I've seen deep blue crevasses and the castle-like suncups that form on glaciers; smelled the sulphur of volcanoes, and the ozone of high altitudes. Today, though, Dad and I are on a simple hike up to the top of Salushkin Falls. We find a place to settle together in the heather meadows and pull out our sandwiches. We sit for a while in companionable silence. Then Dad asks me if there's any song that inspires me. I think about this for a moment. The first Star Wars movie has just come out, and I tell Dad that the Star Wars theme song inspires me. I ask Dad what song inspires him, and he says, without hesitation, "The Lone Prairie."

I am surprised by this. I was expecting him to name some song of the mountains maybe - Dad is a well-known mountaineer, after all, and at the moment we're sitting on the slopes of Rainier.

Intrigued, I ask Dad to sing "The Lone Prairie" for me, and he does - in the same way a young boy might sing to his mother - without artifice or showmanship. It is a sweet moment.

Oh carry me back to the lone prairie
Where the coyotes howl and the wind blows free
And when I die you can bury me
Neath the western skies on the lone prairie...

"Will My Ashes Be with Hers?"
October 3, 2017

Dad and I take a nice drive after school. Not a whole lot of conversation this afternoon - we're both pretty quiet - just looking out at the farmland and the cows, the mountains and the autumn colors. Dad points out the Olympics, Mount Baker, Three Fingers. He talks a little about his work checking wells when he worked for the State - he says he enjoyed that job, traveling around. He talks about the geology of Skagit Valley a little. He asks if he could take a photo of Mount Baker - and I hand him my camera and show him how to zoom in and out. He snaps a quick pic and says he'll maybe use it for a watercolor later. We're both kind of subdued today. He learns - once again - that Moz has passed. That never gets easier for either of us. He asks where she is - and I say her ashes are spread on Alta Vista, on Rainier. He asks, hopefully, "Will my ashes be with hers someday?" - and I tell him yes.

Then, "I love you, Daddy."

"I love you, too. Thank you for the ride today."

"I'm Running for President"
October 11, 2017

I picked Dad up for a drive to Urgent Care this morning. As we're getting him down the stairs and to the car -

Dad: I'm running for President.

Karen: (*Involuntary grin - Dad appears to be in fine form this morning.*) I'd vote for you!

Dad: Do you really think I'd make a good President?

Karen: I think you'd be great!

Dad: (*As we situate him in the car.*) I don't want to bring my walker. I don't think you can be President if you have a walker.

Karen: Roosevelt had polio. He used a brace.

Dad: (*Nodding his head.*) That's true. But he had a lot of people backing him. (*An old receipt starts to work its way out of my car as Dad moves his feet in - I pick up the receipt and shove it back into the car.*)

Dad: I don't think anyone would vote for a President with a messy car.

(*I start laughing.*)

Dad: I wonder how many other old men in this nation are trying to get into a car right now.

As we drive to Urgent Care Dad talks more about his campaign for Presidency.

Dad: I think you should run for President. You're a teacher. What more do you need to be? (*Thinking.*) I wonder how many other daughters are driving their fathers around right now?

I help Dad out of the car and into the waiting room at Urgent Care.

Dad: Do Peter and David know about your attempt to make me President?

(*I shake my head no. I don't really know how to respond to that one.*)

Dad: How do we know when the joke's gone far enough? When do they eliminate me?

Karen: (*I assume Dad's talking about being eliminated from the presidential race - but he's talking really loudly and everyone in the waiting room can hear him, and I don't want there to be any misunderstandings.*) Daddy, no one's going to eliminate you.

We have a wait. Other people who arrived after us have now been called to the back rooms. I ask the receptionist if maybe Dad's been forgotten. She goes to check for me and discovers his chart is missing, and there was some miscommunication somewhere - one nurse thought the other nurse was looking at Dad, and the other nurse thought the first nurse was looking at Dad. Everyone's very apologetic and Dad is quickly brought into the triage room. Soon he's been diagnosed and given a prescription and we are on our way. I stop at Dairy Queen to buy him a root beer float - he has earned it, for sure. He focuses on his float. He's no longer talking about his bid for the Presidency.

I drive him back to his home, and we unload him. I bring a package in with me that his nephew, Brad, sent him and read to Dad the enclosed note from Brad. Brad has sent him a screen dealy that is loaded with a memory card of thousands of pictures taken by Dad. Dad is smiling - really grateful for this gift. I tell him I need to get back to school now.

Dad: Thank you for driving me around this morning.

Karen: I love you, Daddy.

Dad: I love you, too.

"I Didn't Settle Down"
October 22, 2017

I need to go back to Dad's - need to get him to initial some papers. I find him lying on his bed, watching some movie. His face lights up when he recognizes me. He slowly moves himself into an upright position to initial the papers I give him. I hand him a book to use as a make-shift table to sign the papers on. When he's done signing the papers he looks at the book - *Through a Land of Extremes* - and asks me if I've read it. I say no. He says it's a great book, and I sit down next to him on the bed so I can look at it with him. We chat a little then - me talking directly into his ear so he can hear.

Karen: (*Looking at the name of the author on the book cover for Through a Land of Extremes.*) Nick Clinch. He was one of your friends, wasn't he?

Dad: (*Nodding his head*). Yeah.

(*Dad and I look at the book for a while. Then I look up and see Dad's painting of Mount Assiniboine hanging on his wall.*)

Karen: (*Pointing to the painting.*) Is that your favorite painting?

Dad: No. I don't have favorites.

Karen: Were you there when you painted that one?

Dad: (*Looking at the painting and remembering.*) I was climbing in Canada with George Senner and K. We were hiking around from base camp and K told me about this view. It was about a mile from camp.

Karen: (*Pointing to another watercolor.*) What about that one?

Dad: (*Nodding.*) The Picket Range in the North Cascades.

Karen: You have had a really good life, haven't you?

Dad: I really have! Because I didn't settle down.

(*I lean over and kiss the top of Dad's head, and, for a moment, just enjoy the feeling of being near him - of still having him with me.*)

Karen: I love you, Daddy.

Dad: I love you, too. I never dreamed I'd have a daughter like you. Who still wants to visit me and be in contact with me.

(*There's something so touching about the child-like way he says that - there's a sweet innocence in his words - I feel my heart fill up with love.*)

Karen: Well, I have to get back home now.

(*I get off the bed and Dad hands me the book. I start to put it back where I found it, and he says no - he wants me to take it with me.*)

Karen: Bye, Daddy. I love you.

Dad: I love you!

(*I blow him a kiss and he blows me a kiss. I turn off the light...*)

Dad: Hey! Keep my light on!

Church with Moz
October 23, 2017

I take a drive up to Bellingham. I decide to avoid the freeway and stick to the back roads. I have a yearning to meander.

Mindy Jostyn's album, In His Eyes, plays on my CD player as I drive down roads arched and lined in gold. Autumn leaves drift gently down around me. There is no hurry here.

The title song of Jostyn's album begins playing, and I think of Moz as these words fill my car –

"In His eyes, you're a fire that never goes out
A light on the top of a hill
In His eyes you're a poet, a painter, a prophet
With a mission of love to fulfill
Outside there's a world so enchantingly strange
A maze of illusion and lies
But there's never a story that ever could change
The glory of you in His eyes..."

Moz loved that song. When she'd been lying on a hospital bed in my living room – her last day – I'd played Mindy Jostyn's CD for her and I remember how, during that song, she'd gotten quiet and still – her breathing not labored – and her eyes had focused as she listened to the words. There'd been peace in the room.

And there is peace now in my car as the song plays through the speakers. I feel Moz with me. I feel surrounded by her expression of Love.

Listening to Mindy Jostyn's song, I feel Moz and I coming together to have our own church service in my car. Under the golden trees. On a quiet country back road.

"How'd You Like to Think Like a Cow?"
November 2, 2017

As I'm driving to Dad's home I'm thinking about what I'm going to do after I check up on him - I'll drive home, get a fire going in the wood-stove, make myself some comfort food for dinner, and find some mindless show on *Netflex* to watch. It has been a long day.

I find Dad sitting in one of the recliners in front of the TV watching a movie. I lean over and tell him I love him and stroke his forehead. He tells me he loves me, too. He sees I'm just here for a short visit and asks, "You wouldn't want to go for a drive, would you?"

I nod my head and say, "Sure!" Dang. The comfort food and fire in the wood-stove are going to have to wait.

We help Dad get in my car and start on our adventure. Dad says he always enjoys it when we "head for the coast." So I head west.

Dad says I probably know more than he does about what's going on in the world, and asks me if there's any news. I am not sure how to answer this one, but I don't have to because his thoughts move on to something else.

We drive past the place where I usually buy him his root beer floats. It's closed. He looks over to it as we pass and says, "It's closed." I like that he remembers his float-place.

We're driving past green fields full of cows now.

Dad: How'd you like to be a cow?

(*I start laughing.*)

Dad: How'd you like to think like a cow? Wondering when the next feed is coming in. (*Looking at the scenery.*) I've been traveling around this area in the last week. I've been doing field work for people who want to put in irrigation systems.

I head towards Bay View State Park. The lighting on the water is amazing this evening. I park. I've got to take a photo. I tell Dad to stay in the car and grab my camera for some quick pics. As I'm turning back to the car, I see Dad has gotten himself out of the car and is working his way towards me. Oh man. I hurry back to him and turn him back towards the car. He understands that we're going to get back in the car and leave now.

As I'm driving out of the park I thank Dad for wanting to go on a drive tonight. I tell him it's a beautiful night for a drive, and he says, "It really is!"

He wonders how many of his old colleagues from the Water Rights Division at the USGS are still alive - he guesses that he's the only one left. I tell him Fred Beckey died two days ago. I tell him Fred was 94.

Dad: (*Nods his head.*) He always was five years younger than me. I've out-lived all my climbing cronies, but they all out-climbed me.

As I'm heading back towards Dad's home I pass a field full of snow geese. I pull off onto a side road and park so we can watch the geese taking off and swooping in, and listen to them honking to each other. I point to the flock and say, "Snow geese."

Dad: (*Nods his head.*) Yeah. They come in from Alaska. I wonder if they all know each other. I wonder if they tell each other where to go for food. I wonder if you could count them. How many do you think there are?

Karen: There are probably thousands!

(*Dad nods. I head back to Dad's home now.*)

Dad: I really enjoy these little drives we take together.

Karen: Me, too!

(*I pull into Dad's driveway.*)

Dad: Is this where I'm going to eat dinner?

Karen: Yup.

Dad: Are they expecting me?

Karen: Yup.

Dad: (*Entering his home like he's a guest entering a friend's house and holding out his hand to shake Melissa's hand - like he's shaking his hostess's hand.*) Am I late for dinner?

Melissa: No, you're just in time.

Dad: (*Turning to me.*) Thank you for the drive. I love you.

Karen: I love you, too, Daddy.

I'm so glad Dad wanted to go for a drive today.

"We're at Eye Level Now"
November 7, 2017

I stop by to see Dad after work. He's standing up, getting ready to go to bed.

Karen: Hi, Daddy.

Dad: It's my daughter! It's Karen. (*Pause.*) We're at eye level now, aren't we? (I start laughing. It has just occurred to me, too, that Dad is no longer looking down at at my 5'3" from his old 6'0".)

(*Dad sits down on the bed and I sit next to him. I put my arm around him and he shifts a little so he can put his arm around me, too. I rest my head on his shoulder and just enjoy feeling him alive beside me for a few minutes.*)

Karen: Well, I'll go now and let you take your nap.

Dad: Okay.

Karen: I love you.

Dad: I love you, too.

"We Sat on This Bench Before"
November 10, 2017

I call his home to see if Dad is up for an adventure today. Gwen says that Dad has asked her what they have in store for him today - and that he's ready to go for a drive with me.

A while ago Dad lost his last hearing aid. I'm thinking maybe I'll drive him over to my house - I have an old extra hearing aid there - and see if that might help him. On the way to my house we, of course, stop at the Sisters Espresso for his root beer float. His eyes light up when I turn in there, and he nods his head in the affirmative. Courtney asks me if Dad likes chocolate - I say yes - and she gives me a chocolate bar that someone left her to give to any veterans who show up. I give the chocolate and the root beer float to Dad and he happily begins consuming both.

We stop at my house, and I grab the hearing aid and fasten it onto him. He says it helps.

Dad has lately taken to talking about cows. A lot.

Dad: (*As we drive past a field of cows...*) All a cow needs is a dry pasture, grass long enough to eat, and a water supply for drinking.

(*I nod my head.*)

Dad: I like your presence. I like that you ask me to go on these rides with you.

Karen: I like these drives, too, Daddy.

(*We head for Bayview State Park.*)

Dad: This is the way to my former house, isn't it?

Karen: Yes, when you lived in LaConner.

Dad: Are we going to the beach?

Karen: We could do that. (*I turn onto the road to Bayview State Park and park the car near the bench he sat on last time. I come around to help him out of the car.*)

Dad: (*As he heads for the bench...*) We sat on this bench before, didn't we?

Karen: Yes.

Dad: (*He starts to sit down, and then stands back up again.*)
It's breezy today.

Karen: Yes, it is. Do you want to go back and sit in the car?

Dad: Yeah. I don't like breezy.

(*I help him back to the car.*)

As we're driving back to his home, we pass another field of cows.

Dad: I wonder if cows ostracize cows who just stand there and don't eat. (*He starts cracking up, and I'm laughing at the idea of that, too. Tears are pouring down his face.*) I wonder if cows ostracize other cows for refusing to graze... hahahhahahar...

Dad: Thank you for taking me on these drives with you.

Karen: Thank YOU for coming with me.

I pull up alongside the front door to his home and help him inside.

Karen: I love you, Daddy.

Dad: And I love you.

"I'm in a Race Today"
November 12, 2017

Dad was still in bed when we arrived, watching *National Velvet* on his TV.

Dad: I'm in a race today.

Karen: No, it's alright. You don't need to race today.

Dad: But there's a big trophy I need to win.

Karen: No. It's okay. You can stay in bed.

Dad: Stop lying to me. (*He's not saying this like he's angry at me, he's saying this like he thinks I'm trying to make him feel better.*)

(*I leave for a moment and Scott goes in to talk to Dad. When I get back...*)

Dad: Did you get the race postponed?

Karen: Yeah. (*I give Dad the thumbs up.*) It's all okay.

Dad: Thank you.

"I Really Have"
November 16, 2017

Dad's lying in bed watching the end of a Jean Harlowe movie when I come in. He asks me if I know who these people are - I tell him I recognize Jean Harlowe, but not the other woman. He says that's Marie Dressler. I tell him I love old movies. He says he does, too. A short clip comes on after the movie that highlights the career of Cary Grant and we watch that for a while, holding hands, and just being together.

Karen: You've had a good life, haven't you?

Dad: I really have. I have a good family. I love my children.

Karen: And we love YOU.

Dad: And you love each other.

Karen: Yes, we do.

I stay a little longer and then as I get up to leave...

Dad: I love you.

Karen: I love you, too, Daddy.

"This Looks Familiar"
November 18, 2017

Dad is just finishing up his breakfast when I get there. We put shoes on his feet, his alpine hat on his head, and a sweater over his shoulders and load him up in my car for a drive. First stop: Sisters Espresso for his root beer float.

As we're driving through the Skagit flats...

Dad: What kind of bird would you like to be if you were a bird? A seagull?

Karen: Yeah, maybe. (*Thinking*.) Or a kingfisher... those are pretty cool... they dodge up and down and skim the water... how about you?

Dad: (*Thinking*.) A seagull, I guess.

(*We drive along the water for a bit*.)

Dad: How'd you like to be a seabird, just sitting on the water, waiting for your next meal to turn up...

(*On impulse, I turn down the airport road and head towards the little Skagit airport. Every now and then I stop to take pictures of the autumnal trees*.)

Karen: I love autumn!

Dad: (*Nodding his head*...) Yeah. I think my favorite time of year is late October.

(*I discover there's a flight museum at the airport I never knew was there and pull over to take a picture of an old propeller. Dad's turning his head from left to right - checking things out*.)

Dad: I really appreciate you taking me on these scenic drives. Thank you.

Karen: I enjoy these drives.

(*We head back to Dad's home and pull into the driveway*.)

Dad: This looks familiar.

Karen: Yup. You're home!

Dad: Are they expecting me?

Karen: Yes, they are.

Dad: What are their names?

(I tell him the names of the people who care for him, and he nods his head - I think he's trying to remember the names of his hosts, so he can be a good guest.)

I bought Dad a pair of headphones for his television - I'm hoping they can help him hear the dialogue. Gwen and Cindy and I play around with the headphones for a while - trying to get them to work - and we finally find success! I lead Dad to his room and put the headphones on him, and he can hear the conversation on the television. We settle him onto his bed.)

Karen: (*Waving good-bye...*) I love you, Daddy!
Dad: (*Waving back...*) I love you, too!

When Moz Was Still Here
November 22, 2017

*A comforting ritual – baking the annual Thanksgiving
pies connects me to Thanksgivings past – decades
of home and love, laughter, food, memories of those
newly-arrived and departed. This year will be the first
Thanksgiving without Moz, and as I pour blackberries
into the pie I realize these berries were ones I picked
the summer after she passed, and I wonder if I might
have a left-over bag of blackberries I picked during
the summer before – when Moz was still moving amongst
us. I go to the freezer in the garage and root amongst
the frozen bags, digging, searching – and there! I find
a bag of berries marked 2016! And now a part of the world
that still held Moz in it is in this year's Thanksgiving pie.*

"I Always Like to Orient Myself"
December 4, 2017

I ask Dad if he'd like to go for a quick drive. He says yes, he'd like that. So we put shoes on his feet and a sweater over his shoulders and load him up in my car.

Karen: It's good to have you in the car with me again, Daddy.

Dad: I'm lucky to have you in my life.

(*I decide to stick to the back roads and avoid the holiday traffic.*)

Dad: We're heading south. (*We are.*) I always like to orient myself at the start of every drive so if I need to walk home I'll know which direction to go. (*He starts chuckling, and I start chuckling with him - wondering if he's remembering some time when he unexpectedly found himself walking home. Knowing the kind of life Dad has led, I wouldn't be surprised.*)

Dad: What level do you teach now?

Karen: High school.

Dad: Do you like your students?

Karen: I do!

Dad: Do they like you?

Karen: (*Smiling.*) They do!

Dad: Do you like where you live?

Karen: Yes. Do you like where you live?

Dad: I'm not sure where I live anymore.

Karen: That place you just came from - that's your home. (*Dad nods.*)

Dad: I like this area.

Dad: What is the date today?

Karen: December fourth.

Dad: July fourth?

Karen: December fourth.

Dad: December fourth?

Karen: Yes.

(*We turn around and are heading back to his place now. I pull up into his driveway.*)

Dad: Do these people know me here?

Karen: Yes. This is your home. (*Dad nods, accepting this.*) I love you, Daddy.

Dad: I love you, too.

"Do You Know Where You Are?"
December 6, 2017

I stop by to see Dad after work. He's watching TV in the group room and looks up when I come to his side. "Karen!" he says. And then, "Are we going for a drive?" I ask him if he wants to go for a drive, and he says, "Yeah."

They're working on the road in one direction, so I launch us in the opposite direction, and then turn towards Sedro-Woolley.

I meander down by-ways and side roads, trying to avoid the highway. We come upon some trumpeter swans and I point them out to Dad. "Canada geese?" he asks, and I tell him they are trumpeter swans. He says, "I didn't hear any of that. I think I'm losing my hearing." I tell him we're coming into Sedro-Woolley. He asks, "Jo?" I say no, Sedro. He asks, "What? I didn't hear any of that." I tell him that's okay and pat his leg.

Dad: Where are we?
Karen: Sedro-Woolley.
Dad: Where?
Karen: Sedro.
Dad: Sedro-Woolley?
Karen: Yes. (*And I'm so tickled he finally gets it that I want to bring out balloons and party favors and maybe have a parade.*)

I take side streets out of Sedro-Woolley, heading north, trying to keep the sun out of our eyes.

Dad: Do you know where you are?
(*I tilt my hand side-to-side - making that "sort of" gesture - and tell him I'm exploring. I see a snow-covered mountain in front of us and point to it...*)
Karen: Do you know what that mountain is?
Dad: I'm not sure.
Karen: I think maybe that's Sauk Mountain.
Dad: What?
Karen: Sauk Mountain. Remember when we hiked up that?
Dad: Sauk Mountain. Yeah. We hiked up there, didn't we?
Karen: Yes.

Dad: When there wasn't snow on it.

Karen: Yup.

(*We're following behind a school bus now, and I'm thinking it's time to turn around. I pull into a driveway and wait for the cars that were behind us to go past, and then look the other direction. Dad is looking, too...*)

Dad: It's good on the right!

(*And there's something just really cool about the idea that Dad is my teammate on this adventure, helping me watch out for cars.*)

Dad: Thank you for taking me on these little drives. It's nice to get out now and then. I've been on roads I've never seen before.

(*I pat his leg. And then I hold his hand. I say, "I love you, Daddy." And I know he can't hear me, but it doesn't matter. The car is full of love - even if he can't hear me, I know he must feel it.*)

We're heading back towards his home now. For a while we don't talk. And then...

Dad: Where's Mom?

(*I don't know how to answer this.*)

Dad: Is Mom dead?

Karen: Yes.

Dad: She's been gone a long time.

Karen: Yes.

Dad: I miss her. We made a good home together. I wish I could have been there with her when she...

Karen: You told her you loved her, Dad.

(*Dad thinks about this for a while.*)

Dad: What was your favorite home that you lived in with us?

(*I give an answer, but he can't hear me. So I ask him what he considers HIS favorite home.*)

Dad: You mean my favorite home with Mom and you kids? (*Thinks about this.*) There were so many... it's hard to say. (*There were only two homes that we lived in as a family, but I don't say this to Dad.*)

Dad: (*Looking around.*) I bet you've been on a lot of roads today with me you've never been on before.

Karen: (*Laughing.*) I have!

(*As we turn on the street where he lives...*)

Dad: How did you meet these people? (*And I know he's talking about the people who take care of him now.*)

Karen: I feel like Mom brought us to this place. I feel like she led us here - like she knew this would be a good place for you - they've got cats and dogs - and she wanted you in a place where she knew they would take care of you, and love you.

Dad: How did Mom meet these people? Church?

Karen: No... (*I can't explain my feeling that finding this place for Dad was kind of cosmic, and that Mom brought us here...but we're approaching his house now and Dad points to it...*)

Dad: (*Explaining why he recognizes his home...*) It has that built-out wing...

We pull into the driveway, and I get out to help Dad out. I tell him I love him, and he says, "And I love you."

Melissa comes out to help Dad up the stairs and asks him if he had a nice drive.

Dad: Yes, we saw a lot of nice scenery.

We help him into a recliner in the group room, and this time he's the first one to say it...

Dad: I love you.

Karen: I love you, Daddy.

"The Old and the New"
December 9, 2017

Dad has just gotten out of bed and is eating breakfast when I get to his group home about 1:00. I ask him how he's doing, and he says fine.

Dad: I just bought another car.

Karen: Yeah?

Dad: A 1927 or 1928. Chevy sedan.

Karen: Cool! What color is it?

Dad: (*Shrugs.*) I don't know. Tan, I think.

(*I put my hand on top of Dad's hand on the table.*)

Dad: (*Looking at our hands.*) The old and the new.

(*It makes me grin to think of myself as "new" - I don't think many people would think of me as "new" these days. But Dad is 99, so I guess it's all relative.*)

Karen: What are you going to do after lunch?

Dad: I don't know. What do I ever do?

Karen: Are you going to watch old movies?

Dad: Probably. (*Explaining how it's set-up...*) I can lay on my back on my bed and watch movies. There's a TV on the wall.

Karen: That's cool.

Dad: Yeah.

(*For a while we sit quietly with each other while Dad eats his breakfast.*)

Dad: Are you going to take me for a drive today?

Karen: Do you want to go for a drive?

Dad: (*Nods his head.*) Yeah.

After Dad finishes his breakfast, we put his shoes on and a hat on his head, and help him out to the car. He's still wearing his jammies. I head the car west this time, and head for the country.

Dad: What made you think of taking me for a drive today?

Karen: (*Smiling.*) I love you!

Dad: (*Laughing.*) I knew you'd say that!

(*We stop at the Sisters Espresso for Dad's traditional root beer float and a lavender iced tea for me.*)

Karen: You want a root beer float?
Dad: (*Nods his head.*) Yeah!

We drive through the countryside for a bit. We get near a place where we saw a flock of snow geese a couple weeks ago....
Dad: Do birds - geese - come down here from Canada and spend the winter here?
Karen: Yes!
(*As if on cue, I suddenly spot a family of trumpeter swans in a field next to the road, and point them out to Dad.*)
Dad: (*Nods his head.*) Yeah.

We pull up to his home.
Dad: Are you dropping me off here?
Karen: Yup.
Dad: For the night?
Karen: (*Pause.*) This is your home, Daddy.
Dad: (*Frowns.*) Home.
Karen: (*I pat his leg.*) Hold on. I'll come around and help you into the house.
(*I go around the car and help Dad out of it and up the stairs. He needs to use the bathroom, and I help him to the door.*)
Karen: I love you, Daddy.
Dad: I love you!

"Any Problem Getting Through Customs?"
December 15, 2017

Dad: Are we going to have any problem getting through customs?

Karen: We don't need to go through customs.

Dad: But are we going to have problems getting through Canadian customs?

Karen: You live in the United States. I live 15 minutes from you. We don't have to go through customs.

Dad: Oh. That's good.

Karen: I love you.

Dad: I love you!

Winter

I'm 26. In the last few years Dad has met a couple of men I've dated. He has not always been impressed. He shook hands with one of them and observed afterwards that his hand was small and his grip not strong. He noted that another one didn't seem at all interested in the mountains. He agreed with me that one was too religious, and another seemed lacking in integrity.

And then I bring home Scott. I've already pre-checked the important things: He's climbed Mount Baker; I witnessed him open a door for an elderly woman with her hands full; I've observed his keen sense of humor; he has a firm handshake and a full-faced twinkly-eyed smile. He's smart and kind and attractive.

It is Christmas when I invite him to my folks'. Scott brings over a bottle of Kahlua. There's a cork in the bottle that refuses to be pried from its place of honor. Scott yanks. Nothing. Dad yanks. Nothing. The cork will not be moved out of the bottle. Finally the two of them work together and manage to push the cork INTO the bottle. Problem solved. We're all cracking up. We have bonded.

"The Feeling Is Mutual"
December 30, 2017

Dad's just finishing breakfast when I get there. I ask him if he's ready to go for a drive. He says, "But there's something I need to tell you. Karen and Scotty are planning to take me for a drive, too."
Karen: (*Laughing.*) I AM Karen!
Dad: (*Really looking at me.*) Oh.
(*Cindy, one of Dad's care-givers, is grinning. I tell her that THIS is a first for me. I must have aged a lot in the last couple days, I say, and Cindy starts laughing.*)

We help Dad into the car - Dad turns to thank Dietrick, the man who's helping him into his seat - and we head out on today's adventure. I'm hoping to take Dad for a nice long drive today.
Dad: What time are you picking me up tonight to bring me to your house?
Karen: Daddy, Christmas was last week.
Dad: Oh.

We stop at the Sisters' Espresso, and I look over at Dad.
Karen: You want a root beer float?
Dad: (*Nods his head and smiles.*)
(*I go up to order a float for Dad, and bring it back to him - complete with straw and spoon.*)
Dad: Thank you. (*He looks over at me and notices I don't have a drink.*) Did you get yourself anything?
Karen: No, I'm fine.

It occurs to me now that Dad probably wants to see Scott - he's mentioned that he was hoping to come over tonight, and told me that "Karen and Scotty are planning to take me for a drive" - so I decide to make a stop at the house so he can have a quick visit with my husband.

When I get to my home, knowing how difficult it is for Dad to get into and out of the car, I tell him to stay in the auto - and go inside the house to fetch Scott and my youngest son, who is visiting us. Scott and Xander come out to say hi to Dad. Dad grasps Scott's hand in his usual strong grip, and then grasps Xander's hand and notices the tiger-face tattoo on his hand. "Art work!" he says, and asks Xander if he has any tattoos on his chest. Xander laughs and acknowledges that he does.

Scott tells me that there are snow geese in the local elementary school field, and I head out with Dad in search of them. Sure enough - there's a lively flock of snow geese fluttering around in the field next to the school. I park in such a way that we're facing out towards them, and Dad can watch them from the car.

Dad: They come down every winter, don't they?
Karen: Yep.
Dad: Where do they come from?
Karen: Alaska.
Dad: Alaska? (*Nods his head.*)

I know how much Dad has always enjoyed our visits to Bay View State Park, and decide to head there with him. It's cold today, and I'm thinking I probably won't stop at the park with Dad - but it might be nice for him to go through territory familiar to him.

As we approach the park, Dad says, "We've been on that beach before, haven't we?"

And it's a little thing - what he's just said - but it makes me inordinately happy to know that he remembers our visits to the park.

Now I think I'll head out towards Conway - he's always seemed to enjoy that area. But before I get to Conway, I decide, on impulse, to turn down the road Dad once directed me to turn down right after he and Moz moved up here. The road holds a happy memory for me - that day with Day - and I drive along it, remembering when there were blue skies overhead and orange poppies along the roadside. And Moz still alive. Dad has perked up a little, and is scanning the scenery from left to right.

As we pass the nicely-groomed lawns and well-maintained homes...

Dad: This is a company town. Those are the managers' homes.

Karen: (*Sometimes talking with Dad is like doing improv.*) Yeah.

Dad: Am I the only one you go driving around the county with?

Karen: I love going driving with you!

Dad: What?

Karen: (*Louder.*) I. Love. Going. Driving. With. You!

Dad: (*Smiles.*) And I love going driving with you. The feeling is mutual.

We turn around at the end of the road and head back.

Dad: Have you ever been on this road before?

Karen: With you. You directed me here once.

Dad: Oh.

I've got the heat on in the car. As we head back to his home, Dad nods off. He wakes up as we drive along the Skagit River. He takes note of the fishermen, and starts becoming more alert as we near his home. He starts coughing fiercely.

Karen: Are you alright?

Dad: Did you just ask me if I'm alright? (*With conviction...*) I'm okay.

As we pull up into the driveway...

Dad: Am I going to spend the night here?

Karen: Yes. This is your home.

Dad: Oh.

Karen: (*I want to say this before he leaves the car, while it's quiet and while we're close enough to each other for him to hear me.*) Daddy, I love you.

Dad: (*Smiles at me.*) I love you, too.

I come around to help Dad out of the car. This is invariably the hardest part of our drives together. Dad hands me his root beer float and I put it on top of the car. Dad manages to get one foot on the ground, but it's taking a lot of effort for him to turn around in his seat far enough to get his second foot on the ground. He sighs in quiet frustration, and looks up at me. I smile at him, and he grins back at me and shakes his head. He summons the energy he's always been able to summon when he was heading for a summit, and, using my hands as leverage, he manages to set both feet on the ground.

Karen: One. Two. Three. (*Dad knows on "three" I'm going to lift him up under his armpits and he's ready for this, and pushes up to standing on his trusty, old mountaineering legs.*)

Karen: (*I reach up to the top of the car for the root beer float and hand it to Dad.*) Here.

Dad: (*Taking the root beer float from me.*) There's still ice cream in the bottom of it.

I help him into the house and up the stairs. He lets me know he needs to use the bathroom now. Cindy greets me at the top of the stairs and I hand Dad off to her, and let her know he's ready for the restroom. I know he's in good hands.

Dad: (*Half-turning to me.*) Thank you for the drive today.
Karen: Thank you for coming with me!

"That's a Nice Place You Have"
January 6, 2018

Karen: Look at all the people here to see you! There's Joe and Robin and Scott and Pete and Sheila.

Dad: Pete's here?

Karen: Yeah… right there… (*I motion for Peter to come up…*)

(*Pete starts talking to Dad about the drive they took to his home on the Hood Canal a couple months ago…*)

Dad: That's a nice place you have.

Pete: We'll try to get back there again after the winter.

"I Was Trying to Take a Breath up to 20"
January 8, 2018

Dad's in bed when I get there.
Karen: Hi, Daddy!
Dad: Hi, Sweetie. Am I going home now?
Karen: You ARE home.
Dad: Oh. Good.
Karen: How are you doing?
Dad: Oh. Well. I was trying to take a breath up to 20. I'd almost done it, too, and then you walked in. (*Starts grinning.*)
Karen: (*Laughing.*) Sorry!
Dad: Where are you going now?
Karen: I need to get home and take care of the dog.
Dad: (*Nods.*) Thanks for stopping by! I love you.
Karen: I love you, too.

"It Grows on You"
January 12, 2018

Karen: What are you watching?

Dad: *The Price is Right*. Do you ever watch *The Price is Right*? It grows on you.

"I'm Watching Lots of Wonderful Movies Here"
January 16, 2018

Karen: Hi, Daddy!

Dad: Hi, Karen. I'm watching lots of wonderful movies here. Movies about wildlife. It's a series called *Planet Earth*.

Karen: Oh! I love those shows!

Dad: They're really good.

Karen: How are you feeling?

Dad: I feel good. How else should I be feeling? I don't have to do anything but sit here and watch TV.

(The nurse is poking Dad's stomach and asks him if it hurts.)

Dad: No. Should it?

Dietrich brings Dad's mail to me and I hand it to him letter by letter and point out the names of the people who sent them.

Dad: (*Looking at the inscription in the first card I hand him.*) Elliot and Diane. Have you ever met them?

Karen: I have! They're wonderful people.

Dad: Yes, they are. (*Looking at the next card.*) The Hardys. I was with them when they first met each other on the Juneau Icefield. They're a nice couple.

(Soon Dad needs to use the restroom. Before he disappears in there…)

Karen: I love you!

Dad: I love you!

"I Wasn't Really Sleeping"
January 18, 2018

Dad is in his bed, sleeping, when I got to his home. I lean over and kiss him on the cheek and he opens his eyes and says, "My daughter!"

Karen: I'm sorry – I didn't mean to wake you up – I just wanted to kiss your cheek.

Dad: I wasn't really sleeping. I just lie here and think.

Karen: What do you think about?

Dad: I think about my travels and my friends and my mountains. I think about traveling around the equator.

Karen: You have a lot of good memories to think about!

Dad: Yeah, I do.

Karen: I just stopped by to say hi, but I'll let you go back to sleep now. I love you.

Dad: I love you.

(*Dad closes his eyes and goes back to his thoughts.*)

Reminder to self: Build up lots of good memories now so you have good times to re-visit when you reach your sunset years.

"Because That's Where the Poets Come From"
January 21, 2018

Karen: Who are you rooting for?
Dad: New England.
Karen: Why?
Dad: Because that's where the poets come from.

"Are You Going to Dump Me Off Here?"
February 6, 2018

Dad is watching a movie when I get there. I sit down in the chair next to him and we hold hands for a while. When I start getting ready to leave Dad says he wants to go with me.

Dad: I need permission to leave here.

Karen: No, you don't. Do you want to go for a drive?

(Dad nods his head yes, and Melissa helps me get him ready to go. When I open the door to the passenger seat, he looks in my car and says, in surprise, "Hey! It's clean!")

I decide to drive us out towards the Sisters Espresso Stand to see if the flood waters have gone down there. If the waters have gone down and the stand is open I'll buy Dad a root beer float.

Dad: It's not the best weather for a drive.

Karen: Yeah, it's kind of ugly out here, isn't it? *(Pause.)* I love you, Daddy.

Dad: And I love you!

(We pass an eagle sitting in a tree and I point it out to Dad.)

Dad: *(Pondering eagles.)* We never saw any eagles in Los Angeles. Maybe they like this weather better.

(We pass a cool old farmhouse - I'm just about to point it out to Dad and tell him how much I've always liked that house, when Dad notices it on his own.)

Dad: That's a picturesque place!

Karen: Yeah! They moved that here from another place...

Dad: *(Having a hard time hearing.)* What?

Karen: They bought that house for, like, a dollar forty-nine and had it moved out here from another place.

Dad: *(Nodding.)* And held up traffic getting it out here.

Karen: *(Laughing.)* Yup!

(We pass Allen School.)

Dad: Did you used to teach there?

Karen: Yup. And you showed your K2 slideshow to my students there.

Dad: *(Nodding.)* I remember.

The flood waters have gone down around the espresso stand and I see that I can drive in there. I pull in next to the stand.

Karen: I think we need to get you a root beer float.

Dad: (*Nods his head.*) Yeah!

(*I get Dad his root beer float and bring it to him. Dad takes it and thanks me, and starts happily guzzling it.*)

We head back to Dad's home. I pull into the driveway and up to the front door.

Dad: Are you going to dump me off here?

Karen: This is your home, Daddy.

Dad: (*Nods his head.*) Oh.

I help him out of the car, into the house and up the stairs. He sees Melissa and says hi, and asks her if he should go into the living room. She smiles and helps him into one of the lounge chairs.

Karen: I love you, Daddy. Thank you for going on a drive with me.

Dad: I love you, Karen.

(*I head out - turn and blow him one last kiss, and he smiles and waves.*)

"Social History?!"
February 16, 2018

Dad's finishing his breakfast when I get to his home to pick him up for his doctor's appointment. I lean over and shout into his ear that he's going to a doctor's appointment for his eyes now. He nods his head and says he hasn't seen his eye for a while. For some reason this strikes me as funny, and I start cracking up. Dad looks over at me and smiles. He finishes his breakfast, Amanda fetches a jacket for him, and we head out. Before we get to the door, Dad says, "I don't need this thing," and shoves his walker off to the side. I retrieve it and stick it in the back of the car – just in case.

We get Dad situated in the car and then he realizes he doesn't have his hat. Dietrick goes to fetch his alpine hat for him. While he's gone Dad starts thinking about his hat – thinking maybe he didn't bring one to "this place." But I tell him this is home and he has a hat in there, and Dietrick is getting it for him. When Dietrick puts it on his head, Dad thanks him. He has his old mountaineering hat on his head now, and everything's right with the world. We set out on our grand adventure…

Dad: I forgot my wallet! I don't have my ID.
Karen: I have your wallet.
Dad: Oh, good. I don't think there's anything in there, anyway. (*He's right.*)

When we get to the doctor's office I go in to see if it's alright if we wait in the car until it's our turn. (*Sometimes there have been complications when Dad is in a waiting room too long.*) The receptionist smiles and says that would be fine. She just needs to make sure all the information they have on Dad is up-to-date. I read the form she hands me and I sign it for Dad – then I think maybe I should bring it out to him and let him sign it, too – just to keep him from getting too bored out there. I hand him the form. Near the bottom there's a heading called "Social History" – I had no idea what that meant when I saw it, and apparently neither does Dad…
Dad: Social history?!

Karen: (*Laughing.*) Yeah, don't worry about that one. (*I bring the form back in, signed by Dad, and deliver it to the receptionist. I mention that my dad was a little confused by the "social history" question and make some joke about asking Dad about the sororities he belonged to and stuff. The receptionist laughs and tells me she'll come and get us when they're ready for Dad.*)

Dad: (*Waiting in the car.*) I should have brought the book I got from the library.

Karen: What book did you get from the library?

Dad: Oh, one of those books I enjoyed reading when I was a teenager. A book by Joseph Altsheler. A book about the frontier and adventure. (*Thinking.*) Do you have any of my old books?

Karen: Yes! You gave me one that is really precious to me – *The Royal Road to Romance.*

Dad: (*Nodding.*) Yeah. That's the one that got me into adventuring. I still remember the opening line: "May had come at last to Princeton."

(*It tickles me that he still remembers the first line to a book he first read when he was a teenager.*)

The receptionist comes out to get Dad pretty soon and we go in to begin his appointment. The eye-lady takes his blood pressure – she says it's good, and I give Dad the thumbs up. Then she asks Dad to cover his good eye to see if he can see anything out of his bad eye.

The eye-lady: What do you see there?

Dad: I don't see anything! You told me to cover my eye!

(*The eye-lady and I start laughing. The eye-lady covers up Dad's bad eye and sees what tricks he can perform with his good eye. He reads the letters on the wall, and then she brings a card up to him to see how close he can see. He reads the letters he's supposed to read and then starts reading the fine print on the bottom that's meant for the eye people…*)

Dad: "The redistribution of…"

Eye-lady: (*Laughing, she takes the card away from him.*) Okay. That's good.

We go into a second waiting room to wait for the rest of Dad's appointment. There are a lot of really cool people waiting in this room, and I start chatting to them. One of the people in there tells me that he's 90. I shout in Dad's ear that the man next to him – and I point – is 90.

Dad: (*Laughing.*) He's just a kid! I'm 100. (*Dad is 99 – he'll be 100 in a few months – and 99 is hard for anyone in that waiting room to beat.*)

Dad: (*After talking about eyes for a bit.*) It's my hearing that's the worst part of me right now.

(*I hand Dad a travel magazine and he starts flipping through the pages. When he gets to a picture of Machu Picchu he stops.*)

Karen: You've been there.

Dad: (*Nodding.*) Yeah. I've been there. Right at the top. (*He starts pointing out the trail to the top.*) It's a steep trail up to the top.

(*Dad gets called back into the inner office for a check-up by the doctor.*)

Karen: (*Shouting into Dad's ear.*) Dad, this is Dr. Sapenstein.

Dad: Dr. Frankenstein?

Doctor: (*Laughing.*) That'll work.

The check-up's over now and we're back in the car.

Karen: Do you want to get an ice cream float ?

Dad: (*Nodding his head.*) Yeah. I'm lucky to have you.

Karen: I'm lucky to have you.

(*We're driving down Burlington Boulevard, and Dad asks which direction we're heading. I think about this and say I think we're heading north, or maybe east. He mentions Hwy 9 – "runs along the foothills of the Cascades" – and I realize that Burlington Boulevard actually used to be a part of an old highway, but I can't remember what it was called anymore. As I'm thinking about this...*)

Dad: Is this Old Highway 99?

Karen: (*Dad remembers what I'd forgotten.*) Yes!

(*We head towards the place where I usually buy Dad his root beer float - The Sisters Espresso on Chuckanut - and I pull into the parking lot in front of it.*)

Dad: (*Recognizing the espresso place.*) This is the usual place!

(I go up to fetch Dad's root beer float and bring it back to him.)

Dad: Thank you!

(I decide to take Dad on a short drive before I return him home. Dad is thinking – and I know he's going to start sharing whatever comes to his thoughts. I enjoy listening to him...)

Dad: I have the TV on 24 hours a day now. There are some really interesting shows that come up.

Karen: Old movies?

Dad: Not old movies. Shows about everything. I keep it on the same channel and all kinds of shows come up. The Olympics.

We drive down country roads, the windshield wipers pushing aside the drizzle landing on the windows. Snow geese and trumpeter swans flap around in fields of green beside the road.

Dad: When I was young I used to think about what my old age would be like. Back when my mind was clear.

Karen: How did you picture your old age?

Dad: Eating simply. Hobbies. Reading mountaineering history.

Karen: Do you enjoy your life now?

Dad: *(Nodding.)* Yeah. I do. I was lucky – I have a good family. My older sister and younger brother did everything with me. My mother and father took us on drives. I probably saw more of Los Angeles than most people who lived there. My dad worked seven days a week – got up early in the morning and came home late at night, but he found time to take us on drives.

(I drive Dad back home. Dietrick comes out to help Dad into the house. I retrieve the walker – Dad never used it – and follow behind. Dad heads for the lounger in front of the TV. He asks about the Olympics. I kiss his forehead...)

Karen: I love you.

Dad: I love you!

"You Have a Sweet Smiling Face"
March 4, 2018

Dad is finishing breakfast when I get to his place. He asks me if I've seen K recently. K died a while ago. I say no, and shake my head in the negative.

Dad: He's living in a place like I'm living in. He's living in... (*Dad turns to Gwen, his care-giver.*) Does this place extend to the border?

Gwen: (*Smiling.*) The ground extends to the border, yes.

We get Dad in the car, and off he and I go on another adventure. As we're driving on a road near LaConner...

Dad: (*Looking around.*) I used to conduct geologic and water rights surveys out here. (*Thinking.*) I wonder if I'll see Mama soon. (*He looks over at me to see what I have to say about it - I wait...not sure which direction I should take.*) I think they're living in a big retirement place of some kind - a long, low building. (*As we're crossing over Hwy 20...*) This is Highway 20. It crosses over the North Cascades. (*Pause.*) Thank you for taking me on these drives.

Karen: I love these drives.

I drive Dad to the Sisters Espresso to get him his root beer float. He thanks me and starts slurping through his straw. He notes that I never get myself anything - concerned about me - and I assure him I'm fine.

I stop by my house so Scott and Xander can come up to the car window and say hi to Dad. He shakes their hands, and nods his head at them, and we continue on our adventure.

Dad: Do you like your job?

Karen: Yes, I do.

Dad: What do you teach?

Karen: I teach everything: Trigonometry, Geometry, Algebra, History, English, Geology, Biology...

Dad: (*Perks up.*) Geology?

Karen: Yup. Geology.

We pull up to his home, and I go around to help him out of the car. Dad pauses just before he's about to close the car door and looks directly at me.

Dad: I love you.

Karen: I love you, too, Daddy.

Dad: You have a sweet, smiling face.

(*I'm touched by his words, and feel the kindness in them lift me up.*)

Amanda and I help Dad to his recliner. Amanda asks Dad if he had a nice drive and he says yes.

Karen: I love you!

Dad: I love you!

"You've Got 'Em All Covered!"
March 10, 2018

Karen: Do you want to go for a drive?
Dad: That's exactly what I need right now.

Amanda helps me get Dad in the car and we head out on today's adventure. As we pass a nearby retirement village I remember that one of Dad's old friends used to live there. I point to it...

Karen: That's where Norma Johnson used to live.

Dad: Norma Johnson? I haven't heard from her or Bob for a while. Are they still alive?

Karen: Bob died a while ago. I'm not sure about Norma.

Dad: That's the thing about getting old. You stop hearing from your friends. You stop expecting to hear from them anymore. People just quietly die off. I wonder if Bob's still alive...(*I don't say anything - he didn't hear me the first time, and I'm thinking I should just let it pass.*) I'd try to find him, but his name is Bob Johnson. There are a lot of Bob Johnsons. He'd be hard to find. (*Thinking.*) How'd you like to be named Bob Johnson? (*Pause.*) Dee Molenaar - there aren't a lot of Dee Molenaars. (*Turns to me.*) Karen Molenaar. There's a good name. Do you go by Karen Molenaar or Karen...? (*Dad struggles to remember my married name.*)

Karen: I use 'em both. Karen Molenaar Terrell.

Dad: Yeah. That's good. You've got them all covered.

(*We're traveling near LaConner now.*)

Dad: There's the tip of Mount Baker. There's the Olympics. This is a beautiful part of the country.

Karen: Do you remember when we climbed Baker together? You and me and Scott?

Dad: (*Thinking, and then nodding his head.*) Yeah. I remember that.

(*I pull over to take a picture of a field of daffodils. Then we head towards Bow. We get to the top of the hill on Farm to Market Road and I see a place to pull over and take a picture of Baker.*)

Dad: What do you do with all these pictures you take? Do you put them in an album?

Karen: I share them with my friends.

(*Dad nods. We stop again so I can take another picture of Baker. I show the picture I took to Dad. He nods.*)

Dad: That would make a good painting. The farm buildings in the foreground and Mount Baker.

(*As we near the Sisters Espresso...*)

Dad: (*Smiling.*) It's ice cream time.

(*I pull into the Sisters Espresso and go up to order Dad's root beer float and a lavender iced tea for me. I hand Dad his float.*)

Dad: Thank you!

(*We head back to his home now.*)

Dad: Who's taking me back to Seattle tonight?

Karen: I'm taking you home now.

(*Dad's quiet - I'm not sure if he's processing what I just said, or if he didn't hear it. As I drive in front of his home he recognizes it...*)

Dad: (*Smiling.*) Ah, the long house.

(*I pull in front of the front door and reach for his ice cream float - it looks pretty empty.*)

Karen: Are you done with that now?

Dad: No! There's some left.

(*I help him out and into the home. Amanda greets Dad and helps him into the recliner in front of the TV.*)

Karen: I love you!

Dad: I love you!

"I Don't Want to Climb That Mountain Again!"
March 16, 2018

Karen: How are you doing?

Dad: I'm good. I'm watching this movie. (*Nods to the TV.*) Have you ever seen this movie?

Karen: (*Glances at the screen.*) "Cat on a Hot Tin Roof."

Dad: Yeah. I still don't know what the title has to do with the movie.

Karen: (*Chuckling.*) Yeah... (*I'm thinking I could maybe try to explain what I think the title means, but decide not to go that direction, instead...*) We're going to try to get you up to Rainier in a few months.

Dad: (*Groaning.*) No, I'm not climbing that mountain again.

Karen: (*Laughing.*) No, you don't have to climb it. You can just sit in the lodge and look at it.

Dad: Oh. (*Smiling.*) That's better. That sounds good.

Karen: Okay. I need to get home and take care of the dog. (*I lean over and kiss Dad's forehead.*) I love you!

Dad: I love you!

Second Spring

I'm 27 and Dad has his arm linked with mine. I ask him if he's ready, and he gives me a confident nod. We enter the edifice and face the altar. Scott is waiting for me at the end of the aisle, smiling at us. Dad takes the first step - and then we're off! - like a horse in the Preakness, he's racing me down the aisle to my new life. This is not what I'd expected, exactly, but it will work, and I join his pace. Afterwards he's embarrassed. He hadn't meant to go that fast, he explains, but he was so caught up in the moment - so resolved to do his part for me - that he pinned his eyes on the goal and away we went.

I tell him our "walk" down the aisle was absolutely perfect and I wouldn't change a thing.

"Communication Without Words"
March 22, 2018

I pull up a chair next to Dad and hold his hand while he watches the *National Geographic* channel. I squeeze his hand once. He squeezes back once. I squeeze his hand twice. He squeezes my hand twice. He squeezes my hand five times, and I squeeze his hand five times. I smile at him and he smiles back at me. Communication without words. Then...

Karen: I love you, Daddy.

Dad: I love you, Karen. (*It touches me that he uses my name. He remembers it.*)

"When Did I Think It Was?"
April 4, 2018

Dad was resting in his bed when we got there.

Karen: Do you want to go for a drive?

Dad: Yes. Am I allowed to leave here?

Karen: (*Laughing.*) Of course! Are you ready to go?

Dad: Yes!

(*Scotty and I situate Dad in the front passenger seat and I sit behind Dad in the back seat. I reach forward and pat Dad's shoulder and he reaches for my hand and holds it.*)

Scott: Where should we go first?

Karen: Sisters Espresso.

(*Scotty heads for the Sisters Espresso. As we pull into the parking lot…*)

Dad: Good! (*Smiling.*) Karen takes me here all the time when we go on our drives…

(*I order the usual root beer float for Dad, and a couple coffees for Scott and myself. I hand Dad his float through the car window…*)

Dad: Thank you!

Karen: Is it good?

Dad: (*Gives the thumbs up.*)

(*We head out to the daffodil fields.*)

Dad: This is beautiful country. (*Thinking.*) I was stationed here for a while – in the Coast Guard. Have you ever been to the Big Four Inn? They turned it into a Coast Guard place during the war.

Karen: (*To Scott from the back seat.*) We went up there with Dad, remember? The inn burnt down – there was just a foundation there.

Scott: (*Remembering.*) Yeah. (*Turns to Dad.*) We hiked up there together, remember? We went hiking with Pete Schoening to the Ice Caves.

Dad: (*Nods, remembering.*)

Scott: (*Talking to me.*) That was one of the last hikes Pete Schoening went on, wasn't it? Do we still have the picture of Pete with the boys?

Karen: Yes. I think I have it on Facebook.

(*The daffodil fields appear on the right.*)

Karen: (*Pointing.*) Look at the daffodils!

Dad: The field is glowing.

(*Scotty pulls over so I can snap some quick photos.*)

Dad: What are we doing for New Year's tonight?

Karen: It's April. We're looking at the April daffodils.

Dad: Oh. (*Pause.*) When did I think it was?

Karen: I don't know.

Dad: (*To Scott.*) I used to live at the Big Four Inn. Have you ever been to the Big Four Inn? The Coast Guard took it over during the war. Where did you live during the war?

Scott: (*Smiling.*) I didn't live anywhere. I wasn't born, yet.

Dad: (*Starts laughing.*) Oh. Yeah.

(*We pass Tulip Town...*)

Dad: There's going to be a lot of traffic here when the tulips bloom. You'll want to avoid this area when it's tulip time. When do the tulips get ripe?

Scott: Another couple weeks, probably.

Dad: (*Making the observation of an artist.*) It's easier to see things when it's raining. There's not as much shadow.

(*As we reach the turn-around point on our drive...*)

Karen: Wayne said he was going to visit you. Did he stop by?

Dad: Yeah. We had a nice visit.

Karen: Did his wife visit you, too?

Dad: Yeah, she was there, too. It was nice.

Karen: Some more of your friends are going to visit in a couple weeks – Tom Hornbein, Bill Sumner, and Jim Wickwire.

Dad: (*Smiling.*) Good! That gives me something to look forward to!

(*We head for Dad's home, and pass, again, the retirement community where Norma used to live...*)

Karen: Norma used to live there, remember?

Dad: Oh... yeah. We visited her there once, didn't we?

Karen: Yes.

Dad: I think she lived in the house right there – right next to the fence.

Karen: Yes, I think so.

Dad: This was the best time to go for a drive. I wouldn't want to be driving around on a weekend when the tulips are blooming.

Karen: This was a nice drive, wasn't it?

Dad: Yes, it was. A nice drive.

(*We turn into the driveway of Dad's home.*)

Dad: I recognize this place. There's that long bedroom…

(*We help Dad out of the car, up the stairs, and into Moz's old recliner in the living room.*)

Karen: Thank you for going on a drive with us, Daddy.

Dad: Thank you for the drive!

Karen: I love you, Daddy.

Dad: I love you!

"Do I Live in a Care Center?"
April 8, 2018

I stop by to see Dad. He wants to go for a drive, so we load him in the car and buckle him up. This time I head for Sedro-Woolley.

Dad: Does this town have a name?

Karen: Sedro-Woolley.

Dad: What? I can't hear you.

Karen: (*I pull into a parking lot and write down "Sedro-Woolley" on a receipt lying in my car, and show it to Dad.*) Scotty and I used to live here. Years ago.

Dad: Did we ever visit you here?

Karen: Yes, a couple of times. (*I drive down to Riverside Park - I want to tell him that this is one of my favorite parks, and that our good friend, a landscape architect, created this park, but I know he won't be able to hear me, and might not understand even if he does. So I don't try to explain. I mentally salute Laurie as we drive past her park. I point to the river...*) There's the Skagit River.

Dad: (*Glances over.*) Does it ever flood over the road?

Karen: I think it might sometimes. Really rarely.

(*I drive past our old house - it is not looking so good these days. I point it out to Dad. He asks if we used to live in one of those houses, and I nod my head, but then quickly drive on. I'm embarrassed by our old house, and sad for it - sad for what it's become. It used to be dear to us. I drive to Dairy Queen, and ask Dad if he'd like a root beer float.*)

Dad:(*Nods his head.*) Yes! Thank you!

Dad has his root beer float now and I head back to his house. We're passing road signs - one of them says, "Life Care Center" and I wonder if Dad has noticed it. He has...

Dad: Do I live in a care center?

Karen: Yes. (*Pause.*) You live in an adult family home.

Dad: (*Leaning over to hear - this is important to him.*) What did you say?

Karen: You live in an adult family home. (*I can feel Dad trying to process this information.*)

(*We pull into the driveway and next to the home's door.*)

Dad: Is this where I'm going to get out now? Will you pick me up from here tonight?

Karen: This is your home, Daddy. This is where you live.

Dad: (*Understanding.*) This is where I live?

Karen: Yes.

Dad: Why are you laughing?

Karen: I'm not laughing. I'm smiling at you. Because I love you. I'm proud to be your daughter.

Dad: I'm proud to be your father.

(*Dad starts unbuckling himself and getting ready to go into the house. I come around to help him.*)

Amanda helps situate Dad in his chair in front of the television.

Karen: Thank you for the drive, Daddy.

Dad: Thank YOU for the drive!

Karen: I love you.

Dad: I love YOU!

"I Don't Think I'm Allowed to Leave Here"
April 12, 2018

I stop by to see Dad after work. The plan is to quickly go in, give him a hug, tell him I love him, and go home. I am looking forward to taking the dog for a short walk, and then settling in front of the TV, watching a British murder mystery and drinking tea...

Karen: Hi, Dad!

Dad: (*Eyes lighting up and a smile coming to his face.*) Hi, Karen! Where are you taking me today?

Karen: (*Pause.*) Do you want to go for a drive?

Dad: Yes, I would! I don't think I'm allowed to leave here, though.

Karen: (*Laughing.*) Of course you are! You aren't a prisoner here.

Amanda: (*Laughing and yelling in his ear.*) You're not a prisoner here. You can leave as long as you're with Karen.

Dad: Okay.

(*We get his shoes on his feet, put him into his sweater, slap his alpine hat on his head, and help him into my car.*)

We head out of town...

Dad: What are we doing for New Year's tonight?

Karen: Dad, you see the blossoms on the trees?

Dad: Yes.

Karen: It's April.

Dad: (*Nods his head.*) We're heading north. (*Thinking.*) Where are we going?

Karen: I'm going to get you a root beer float.

Dad: What? I can't hear what you said.

Karen: (*Louder.*) I'm going to get you a root beer float.

Dad: Ohhhhh! Good! I hope you get yourself one, too. (*Looking out the window.*) This is beautiful country. What are we doing for New Year's tonight? (*I don't know how to answer this, so I don't say anything, and Dad doesn't ask again.*)

We pull into Sisters Espresso and I order a root beer float for Dad and a small shake for myself. While we're there I introduce Dad to Wick, 88, a former big-time rodeo cowboy. Wick's eyes light up when I tell him Dad is going to turn 100 in a couple months. He has found someone older than him. He has a chat with Dad while I wait for my shake.

Dad: (*Slurping on his root beer float.*) Thank you!

(*We drive around for a bit, meandering around the countryside, and then head back to his home. We pull into the driveway...*)

Dad: When will I see you again?

Karen: In two days Tom Hornbein, Bill Sumner, and Jim Wickwire are going to visit you. And I'll be there, too!

Dad: Wonderful!

(*We help him up the stairs. At the top of the stairs...*)

Dad: When will I see you again?

Karen: In two days.

Dad: (*Smiling.*) In two days. Good.

Karen: I love you, Daddy.

Dad: I love you, too!

Epic Afternoon
April 14, 2018

Epic afternoon. Dad was visited by his old mountaineering buddies: Tom Hornbein, Jim Wickwire, and Bill Sumner - extraordinary climbers all. Dad arm-wrestled Tom (Tom and Willi Unsoeld were the first men to ascend Everest from the West ridge); looked at a K2 book with Jim (Jim and Louis Reichardt were the first Americans to ascend K2); and had a good laugh with Bill (who was a member of the expedition that included the first one-legged person to reach the top of Denali). They talked about old friends, old climbs, and the Mountaineers Lifetime Achievement Award Tom is going to receive tonight. (Tom picked up the award for Dad last spring when Dad was in the hospital, and says that helped him prepare for accepting his own award tonight.)

"What Are We Doing for New Year's?"
April 22, 2018

Dad: I don't think I can leave here. I'm being treated for a medical condition.

Karen: It's okay to leave. Do you want to go for a drive with me?

Dad: Okay.

As we're heading out of town a coal train just begins its journey across the road. How long does it take a coal train to cross the road, you ask? This one took about five minutes. A line built-up behind us. When our line of cars started moving, I motioned for the driver who was trying to back-out of a parking space on the side of the road to go ahead and back out in front of me - but hurry, hurry! The driver quickly maneuvered into the line in front of me. The passenger waved at me, and I waved back. Dad was watching...

Dad: Do you know those people?

Karen: No. I was just letting them out of their parking space.

Dad: Oh.

(*We stop for Dad's root beer float at the Sister's Espresso.*)

Dad: Thank you! Are we going to your house for New Year's tonight?

(*Realizing Dad has slipped back to New Year's again, it occurs to me that he never came over to our house for New Year's this year - and maybe I need to bring him to our home. I bring him to our house and park in the driveway...*)

Karen: Do you want to go inside?

Dad: Sure!

I help Dad inside and the youngest son joins us at the dining room table. He chats with his grandpa while I go upstairs to fetch my husband. All together at the table we talk for a while about jobs and vacations and so forth. Then Scotty goes up to get the copy of the *Skagit Valley Herald* that has a picture of Dad and his friends in it, and brings it to Dad. Dad smiles when he sees it, and asks if he can keep it. We tell him that of course he can keep it. When Dad finishes his root beer float I load him back up in the car for the drive back to his place. I help him inside, and Amanda takes him to his chair in the living room.

Karen: Thank you for the drive, Daddy!
Dad: Thank YOU!
Karen: I love you.
Dad: And I love you.

"I've Been Out of It for Months"
April 26, 2018

Dad is lying in bed when I get to his place. I go in and kiss his forehead and ask him how he's doing. He waves his hand toward the television and says, "This is how I'm doing."

Dad: What are we doing tonight for New Year's?

Karen: It's April. (*I go to get his calendar and point out the day to him.*) It's April 26th.

Dad: It's April? I've been out for months!

"More Painless Than I Thought It'd Be"
April 28, 2018

When I get to Dad's place I learn a friend had just sent him
the obituary for author Ruth Kirk. Ruth had been a dear friend of
Dad's and he has tears in his eyes. He is having a hard time of it.
He'd told Megan, his care-giver, that he'd illustrated some of Ruth's
books, and Megan had tried to find one of Ruth's books on Dad's
bookshelves - but hadn't been able to find one - so, instead, she'd
pulled out Dad's book, *The Challenge of Rainier*. They're looking
through Dad's illustrations in his book when I get there.

His care-giver makes room for me to sit next to Dad so we
can talk. Dad shares how sad he is about losing his friend, Ruth. I
tell him that this had been a rough year, and we talk about other
friends he's lost. He says at this point whenever he gets a card in the
mail he expects to find an obituary for one of his friends inside it.

Some people he remembers are gone - climber Fred Beckey,
and his brother, K (although he thought K had just passed away a
couple years ago, when actually he's been gone since 1994). He's
surprised to learn that other friends are gone - "I wondered why I
hadn't heard from them," he says. I think he's wondering why no one
has told him about his friends' passing - so I let him know that we've
shared these passages with him, but that he's forgotten. I suggest that
maybe he forgets because it's too traumatic for him to process - and I
tell him that would be understandable. He seems to accept this.

I always follow my intuition in these conversations -
sometimes I don't bring up Mom's passing, and sometimes - like
today - it seems the right time to talk about it. I know talking about
Mom's passing is very hard for him - but... there are times when I
think it's helpful to him, too. So I hold his hand and share with him,
again, Mom's last week with us - I tell him that he'd been able to say
good bye to her in the hospital before they brought her to my home;
tell him she'd died peacefully in her sleep while I slept on the couch
next to her; tell him I felt her presence brush past me as she left - I
felt her love and joy. I tell him that she'd loved him very much - that
she still loves him - and that we'd promised her we'd take care of
him. Dad nods and weeps quietly as I share Mom's passing with him.

I observe to him that when you live to be 100 you lose a lot of people along the way. "But fortunately," I say, "you have a lot of friends who are younger than you." He smiles and nods.

I ask him if he'd ever expected to live to be 100. He says he'd never thought about it.

Then - "Is it time for a drive?" he asks, hopefully. So his care-givers help me get him ready - get him in his sweater, put shoes on his feet - and I put his alpine hat on his head - and we load him up in my car. I ask him if he'd like me to take him for a root beer float, and he nods his head.

On the drive to the Sisters Espresso...

Dad: I've been thinking this week that I needed to get out of here and get back home to Mom. But now I realize she's gone.

Karen: Yeah. That place where you're living is your home now.

As we turn onto old Hwy 99...

Dad: Now we're heading north. Parallel to the Pacific coast.

Karen: Yup.

Dad: How are the boys?

Karen: They're both graduated from university now.

Dad: (*Taking this in.*) Time goes fast. I was in school a lot longer than them. Or... that's how it feels, anyway.

(*As we turn onto Chuckanut Drive...*)

Dad: Last month when I thought I was dying I was surprised by how painless it was. It's just getting sleepy...

Karen: You thought you were dying last month?

Dad: What?

Karen: (*Louder.*) You thought you were dying last month?

Dad: What? I can't hear you. Let's talk when we get to where we're going.

I pull into the Sisters Espresso...

Dad: (*Smiling.*) I remember this place!

Karen: (*Turning off the car and speaking into Dad's ear.*) Did you think you were dying last month?

Dad: I dreamed I was. I was surprised by how painless it was. It was just like going to sleep.

Karen: Do you feel like you're dying now?

Dad: No. I'm good.

Karen: Good!

(*I get him his root beer float and hand it to him. He thanks me and begins drinking it. I head the car back to his home. As we pass a field bursting with little yellow flowers...*)

Karen: I love you, Daddy. (*I'm not sure he can hear me, but I feel the need to say it.*)

Dad: (*Turning to me.*) And I love you!

We pull into the driveway and next to the front door, and I help Dad get out of the car and up the stairs. The care-giver helps him get situated in the living room in Mom's old chair.

Karen: I love you, Daddy.

Dad: I love you! Thank you!

Karen: Thank YOU!

"Do You Like Picking Me Up?"
May 5, 2018

I drop by to see if Dad wants to go for a drive today. He's sitting at the table finishing breakfast when I get there. He's already dressed and wearing his jacket. His care-giver tells me he was already up and dressed when she went into his room to check on him this morning. I ask him if he'd like to go for a drive. He says yes, and pretty soon he's in my car and ready for an adventure.

There's something I've been meaning to ask Dad. I decide to ask him before I start the car - maybe it'll be easier for him to hear me...

Karen: Dad, how did your parents get to California?

Dad: By way of Holland. Dad came from Amsterdam. Mom came from Rotterdam, I think.

Karen: But once they landed on Ellis Island, how did they come across the country to California? Did they take the train...?

Dad: I doubt it. (*Thinking.*) I never asked them.

(*I start the car and head out on our drive.*)

Dad: It's a beautiful day for a drive. Do we really need to be back in 45 minutes?

Karen: (*I'm not sure where he got that idea. But I reassure him...*) Nope. We can wander and meander and take our time.

Dad: I really enjoy taking these drives with you. Do you like picking me up?

Karen: I love picking you up!

Dad: I love being picked up. (*Looking around at his surroundings.*) The flood plains. (*He sees an emergency veterinarian place.*) Emergency Center. That's where people gather when there's a flood.

We drive out into the country near LaConner. We're driving east.

Dad: (*Looking east.*) Is that Mount Baker there?

Karen: No, Mount Baker is behind you. (*I realize Dad is confused and determine to head north towards Bay View so Dad can see the mountain. After I turn the car north, I point to the top of Mount Baker, peeking over the hills on the right.*) There's Mount Baker.

Dad: (*Nodding.*) Mount Baker. (*His eyes stay focused on the mountain.*) I wonder how many of the people who live here have climbed that mountain. How many times have you climbed Baker?

Karen: Once.

Dad: With me?

Karen: (*Smiling.*) Yup. Once, with you.

Dad: The people who live here are lowlanders. Lowlanders like broad, open spaces. I bet a lot of Hollanders live here. (*Thinking.*) I bet a lot of Dutch people in the Netherlands talk about the Skagit flats.

We cross over Highway 20 and drive along the shore near Padilla Bay. I turn into Bay View State Park and park the car next to the water. I roll down the windows. Dad unfastens his seat belt, as if he's going to get out, but I tell him we're just going to be here for a moment - I want to smell the saltwater. He nods and breathes in the briny air. After a few minutes I roll the windows back up and head out of the park. When I stop to turn right onto the road the car starts beeping at me. Someone is not wearing his seat belt.

Karen: We need to get your seat belt back on you...

Dad: Oh yeah. (*Buckling himself in.*) I'm glad you're concerned about safety. (*Smiling.*) Someone taught you well.

Karen: (*Laughing.*) Yes. Someone did.

(*We get to the other side of the hill and Mount Baker appears - majestic and craggly above the foreground.*)

Karen: Now THAT's a mountain!

Dad: (*Nodding.*) Yeaaaah. (*Looking around him.*) I went bike-riding on this road before. When I was visiting you...

Karen: Yup! You did!

Dad: (*Musing.*) It brings peace to drive along these roads.

Karen: Yes.

Dad: (*Thinking.*) Do I have any unfinished paintings at your house? The last paintings I've done at your house I was just playing around.

Karen: Maybe we can bring you over soon to work on some more.

I turn in at the Sisters Espresso for a root beer float and a breakfast muffin for Dad.

Dad: (*Nodding his head in approval.*) The usual place.

We drive back to Dad's home. I help him into the house, and into his recliner in the living room. He settles into his chair with a huge sigh of satisfaction.

Karen: Thank you for the drive today, Dad.

Dad: Thank YOU!

Karen: I love you.

Dad: I love YOU!

"Can I Fart in Here?"
May 10, 2018

On the way to Dad's eye appointment...

Dad: I don't think I have all the papers I need to provide to the doctor.

Karen: I have them!

Dad: You have them? You're taking care of everything. You're very efficient. Are you efficient as a teacher, too?

Karen: I am!

Dad: Do you like your kids?

Karen: I do!

We get to the doctor's office and Dad stays in the car while I go in to let them know we're there. The receptionist says she'll come out and get us when they're ready for Dad.

While Dad and I are waiting in the car I reach out and hold his hand. We sit in companionable silence for a while. Then I squeeze his hand once, and he squeezes my hand back. He squeezes my hand twice, and I squeeze his hand twice. He squeezes three times and I answer with three squeezes. He squeezes four times and I squeeze back four times. He squeezes my hand five times and I squeeze his hand five times, and then I start laughing. Dad's grinning.

A nice woman in a smock comes out to fetch Dad and leads him right into the room where she checks his vision. I yell into Dad's ear to give him directions from the lady in the smock. "She's going to take your blood pressure now. Now she wants you to cover your right eye. Now your left. She wants you to lean your head back now..." And Dad hands me his old alpine hat for safe-keeping and quietly does what's asked of him.

Now they lead him to another room where they take photos of his eyes. And from there they lead us to a back room where the doctor will examine him. I prepare Dad for the doctor while we wait...

Karen: (*Remembering that last time Dad called the doctor "Dr. Frankenstein."*) Your doctor's name is Dr. Sapenstein.

Dad: Sappenson?

Karen: Sapenstein.

Dad: Sapenstein?

Karen: Yes.

Dad: (*Thinking.*) Can I fart in here?

Karen: (*Laughing.*) No! Wait until you get back out to the car.

Dad: (*Grinning.*) But you'll be in the car, too.

Karen: (*Laughing.*) Yeah. But that's okay.

The doctor comes in and looks at the photos of Dad's eyes. Dad was already pretty much blind in his right eye, and the doctor says his left eye has gotten worse since the last time we were in. He says they're going to need to inject some medicine in his eye.

Karen: Dad, they're going to inject some medicine in your eye. Some of my friends have had this procedure. It's painless and very quick. It's no big deal. You were on the 1953 K2 Expedition. This will be nothing to you.

Dr. Sapenstein: He was on the 1953 K2 Expedition? Did they summit?

Karen: No. This is the expedition that was famous for The Belay. My dad was one of the danglers on The Belay. I wouldn't be here if it wasn't for The Belay. Dad is in *Wikipedia*.

Doctor: (*Nodding his head, and looking at Dad's name on the screen again.*) I know him!

Karen: Yup. He's pretty amazing. The last mountain we were on together was Mount Adams. Dad was 80. I was 40. Dad got to about 10,000 feet and said he was holding us all back and stopped there. It's the first mountain I ever summited without Dad. And it's the last big mountain I ever climbed. But we climbed Rainier and Hood and Baker together. Do you climb?

Doctor: I used to...

(*The doctor leaves and a technician comes in and out a few times to get Dad ready for the procedure. During one of the times we're alone...*)

Karen: We're going to get you up to Rainier to see your mountain again in a month when you turn 100.

Dad: Who's "we"?

Karen: Your family and friends.

Dad: Good! I was going to do that anyway...

The doctor comes back and I stop talking while the doctor gets ready to inject the medicine into Dad's eyeball. I figure the doctor needs to be able to concentrate on what he's doing. After he's done with the procedure, the doctor continues...

Doctor: Did you ever meet Ake and Bronka Sundstrom? They were both in their eighties and climbed to Camp Muir every week...

Karen: Yes. I've met them. I know who you're talking about. Dad was friends with them.

Doctor: Well, after Ake died I climbed with Bronka to Muir.

Karen: How did you meet Bronka?

Doctor: I climbed Rainier about ten years ago and on the way down I saw this older couple on their way to Muir. It was Ake and Bronka. Later I was introduced to Bronka because I'm Jewish and Bronka is Jewish - she's a concentration camp survivor. And I climbed to Muir with her.

(*I want Dad to know about this so I yell into his ear...*)

Karen: Dad, you remember Ake and Bronka?

Dad: (*Nodding.*) Ake and Bronka?

Karen: Yeah. Your doctor climbed to Camp Muir with Bronka after Ake died.

Dad: Ake died?

Karen: Yes. (*I can see Dad becoming sad. I'm sure at one point he was told about Ake's death - but he forgets these passings of old friends, and the grief hits him like a new thing. I turn to the doctor and ask if Bronka is still alive, and he says yes.*) But Bronka's still alive. (*Dad nods his head*). Your doctor is a climber, too.

Doctor: I'm a climber, but I'm not anywhere near your league.

(*Dad starts laughing.*)

Karen: (*To the doctor.*) Yeah. He got that one. (*Doctor starts laughing.*)

Doctor: His eyesight should improve now. I think we got this early enough that it will make a difference.

Karen: (*Yelling in Dad's ear.*) Your eyesight should get better now. This medicine should help.

As I'm making another appointment for Dad, he heads out to the car. Back in the car...

Karen: Do you want to get a root beer float?

Dad: Yeah. The usual place?

Karen: Yeah.

Karen: I love you, Daddy.

Dad: I love you.

"Did You Feel the Bench Vibrate?"
May 14, 2018

It's a beautiful May day - warm and sunny - and I decide that this is the day I will finally get Dad up to Boulevard Park in Bellingham. The last couple times I've tried to get Dad into the park I haven't been able to find an empty parking space. I'm hoping today I will.

As we're driving up I-5 to Bellingham...

Dad: Where are we going?

Karen: Bellingham.

Dad: What?

Karen: Bellingham.

Dad: What? I can't hear you.

Karen: Hold on. (*I realize it's going to be difficult to talk to Dad in the car. But we'll be in Bellingham soon, and he'll see for himself where we're going.*)

Dad: (*Thinking.*) Have you seen Mom lately?

Karen: (*I'm not sure which direction to go with this question. It's going to be very difficult to have a conversation about Mom in the car - we'll be yelling back and forth to each other and he won't be able to hear me. So I decide pithy might be the way to go here.*) No.

Dad: (*Thinking.*) Lake Samish should be off to the left somewhere... (*Dad's right - we're passing the lake right now.*)

Karen: (*Yelling.*) Yes. It's right down there.

Dad: (*Nodding.*) Ten thousand years ago this area was covered in glaciers.

Karen: Yup!

(*We exit the freeway into Bellingham.*)

Dad: (*Reading a sign.*) Fairhaven. Where are we going?

Karen: Boulevard Park.

Dad: What?

Karen: Boulevard Park.

I turn into the park and begin my quest for a parking space. Every space has a car in it. Every space except the handicapped spaces, anyway. Dad will be a hundred next month and relies on a walker - I suppose I could get a handicapped permit for him - but I've never bothered to do that. I pull into a handicapped space just for a second and roll down the windows - I just want Dad to be able to smell the salty air coming off the bay. Dad starts to get out of the car, but I motion for him to stay in his seat.

Karen: I'm parked in a handicapped space and we can't stay here. I just wanted you to see the park for a moment.

Dad: (*Nodding.*) Okay.

I pull out of the space and start to head for the exit, but just then a woman heads for her car. She looks at me and smiles. I mouth the words, "Are you leaving?" And she nods her head. We have found a parking space! And it's even closer than the handicapped space to the nearest bench! I park and help Dad get out of the car. We head for the bench.

Karen: Are you hungry?

Dad: Yeah. And thirsty.

Karen: I'm going to go into the little coffee shop and get you something to drink and eat.

Dad: (*Nods.*) Okay.

Karen: Stay here.

Dad: Okay.

(*I order Dad his favorite kind of milkshake - vanilla - and a bran muffin and get myself a small mocha. I periodically look out the window to see if he's still on the bench.*)

Karen: (*Handing Dad his muffin and drink.*) Here, Dad. A vanilla milkshake.

Dad: Thank you.

(*We sit for a while and watch the boats and kayaks on the bay. Then Dad indicates he wants to move out of the shade so we make our way to another bench that will get him into the sunshine.*)

Karen: Do you see the paddle-boarder?

Dad: (*Eyes on the bay.*) Yeah. I'd rather be sitting down on the board. (*Dad watches a dog waiting for his human outside the coffee place.*) That's a pretty dog.

Karen: Yes, he is!

(*Pretty soon the dog's human comes out to give him water. This dog is one of the calmest dogs I've ever seen.*)

Karen: (*To the dog's human...*) That's a really cool dog!

Dog's human: Yes, he is! He's very chill.

Karen: What's his name?

Dog's human: Titan. (*Laughing.*) And that name so doesn't fit him.

Karen: He should be named after the god of sleep or something.

Dog's human: (*Laughing.*) Yeah, really.

(*I point out the Canadian Coastal mountains to Dad.*)

Dad: That's Canada over there?

Karen: Yup.

(*I point out a kayaker to Dad and ask him if he's ever kayaked.*)

Dad: I think I was out on that water once a few years ago. For a few hours. I got bored...

Karen: (*Laughing.*) Do you see the piers over there?

Dad: Yeah. What are the piers for?

Karen: That's the Alaska Ferry terminal. You gave a talk there once. Do you remember?

Dad: (*Thinking.*) Huh. (*Looking around.*) This is a nice park. Is it a state park?

Karen: I think it's a city park.

Dad: It's nice. What's it called?

Karen: Boulevard Park.

(*Dad nods. I feel the bench underneath me vibrate, and start laughing.*)

Dad: (*Laughing with me.*) Did you feel that? Did you feel the vibration?

Karen: (*Nodding and laughing.*)

Dad: I farted. (*There are few things that give Dad as much pleasure as his own farts.*) We have a new home. I'd like to see it.

Karen: Do you want to go home now?

Dad: (*Nodding.*) Yes.

(*I make to help Dad get off the bench.*)

Dad: No, I don't need help. I'm not a cripple. I can get up on my own.

Karen: Okay.

(*We make our way back to the car and head out of the park.*)

Dad: Boulder Park. It was probably named for all the boulders on the beach.

(*I don't correct Dad. Boulder Park seems as good a name as Boulevard Park.*)

Dad: Thank you for taking me on this drive.

Karen: I'm enjoying it.

Dad: I haven't seen Mom for a while.

Karen: (*Trying to figure out how to respond...*) Daddy, Mom passed on a year ago.

(*Dad doesn't respond and I'm not sure he heard me.*)

Dad: We need to move closer to you.

Karen: I live 15 minutes away from you.

Dad: Thank you for driving all the way down to my home to pick me up for this drive today.

Karen: (*I'm not sure where Dad thinks he lives - so I just nod my head.*) No problem.

(*We pull into his driveway and park in front of the door to the adult family home.*)

Karen: Thank you for coming on a drive with me today. Did you enjoy it?

Dad: I enjoyed it very much.

Karen: I love you, Daddy.

Dad: I love you.

"I've Been Here a Year?!"
May 21, 2018

Dad is in bed watching TV when I get there. He looks over at me when I walk into his room and his face lights up...

Dad: Weeeeellllll! How wonderful to see you!!! (*He reaches out and gives me a tight hug.*) I sure love you!

Karen: I love you, too!

Dad: Thank you for decorating my room for me! (*He gestures around the room.*) When did you do this?

Karen: Pete and Dave and I decorated your room for you a year ago when you moved in.

Dad: I've been here a year?!

Karen: Yup.

Dad: I'd like to go home now.

Karen: You are home, Daddy. This is your home and these people take care of you and love you.

Dad: (*Pointing to the TV where an old black-and-white movie is playing.*) I'm watching this show on TV. I don't know - it might be part of the program here.

Karen: (*Looking at the TV.*) You're watching the old movie channel.

Dad: Oh.

Karen: I wanted to stop by on my way home from school to check up on you. How are you feeling? Are you feeling happy and healthy?

Dad: (*Nodding.*) I'm happy and healthy.

Karen: (*Kissing Dad's forehead.*) I love you.

Dad: I love you. You're wonderful! When will I see you again?

Karen: Maybe tomorrow or the next day. I'll stop by and see you soon.

Dad: (*Nodding his head.*) Okay.

Karen: (*Blowing a kiss.*) Bye, Daddy! I love you!

Dad: (*Waving.*) I love you!

"Who's We?"
May 22, 2018

Dad is in bed when I get there, napping. I stroke his forehead and he opens his eyes.

Dad: (*Reaching up to hug me.*) I love you!

Karen: I love you, too. (*Speaking into his ear.*) I brought my phone in so I could show you pictures of Claire's wedding.

Dad: I was there, wasn't I?

Karen: No, it happened last weekend. I have pictures to show you.

Dad: Good.

Karen: There's Claire and Michael...

Dad: They're a nice-looking couple.

Karen: Yes! And there's Casey - he sang a song at the wedding. And here's Alexander and Claire and Andrew. My sons are all grown-up now...

Dad: (*Trying to bring the phone closer so he can see.*) I prefer to look at regular photos.

Karen: I'll bring some in the next time I come, okay?

Dad: Yeah. When will I see you again?

Karen: Maybe tomorrow or the next day. I'll come back soon.

Dad: Good. I love you!

Karen: I love you, too!

Dad: What are we doing for New Year's?

Karen: (*Speaking into his ear.*) This is May 22nd. Your birthday's in a month. We're going to try to get you up to Rainier for your birthday.

Dad: Who's we?

Karen: Your family and friends.

Dad: Good. Up to Paradise?

Karen: Yes.

Dad: Good!

Karen: Bye, Daddy! I love you!

Dad: I love you!

"I've Climbed up to the M"
May 24, 2018

Dad was sitting at the table eating a meal when I got there. His eyes were closed and his head was slumped over - he appeared to be resting between bites. Eating is hard work when you're 99 and 11 months.

I sat down on a chair next to him. He opened his eyes and smiled. "Well! Hello!"

Karen: Hi, Daddy. I brought pictures of Claire's wedding. (*I bring out the sheets of wedding photos for Dad.*)

Dad: Oh! (*He looks at the first picture - a photo of the University of Montana campus with the big "M" on the hillside in the background.*) I've been there! (*Of course he has, right?*) I climbed up to that big M. (*He traces the trail up to the M with his finger.*) Was the wedding on the campus?

Karen: No. They got married at a ranch. Here's a picture of Claire and Michael...

Dad: A nice-looking couple.

Karen: And do you know who this is?

Dad: (*Nodding his head, thinking.*) Yes.

Karen: Yeah. That's Casey singing a song. He sang a song for Claire and Michael.

Dad: Oh.

Karen: And here's Scotty and David. And here's Casey and Andrew and Xander. (*Dad nods.*) And there's Claire and Casey and Andrew and Xander - all your grandchildren - they're all grown-up now!

(*Dad gives a kind of a tragic moan - and I know he's wondering how he missed their growing up - where the time went.*)

Dad: Were you there?

Karen: Yes. See - here're Claire and me together.

Dad: When was this?

Karen: Last weekend.

Dad: You were in Montana last weekend?

Karen: Yes. (*And I feel... I'm not sure... remorse maybe - that Dad couldn't be there with us, too. I suddenly find myself filled with a deep sadness. I lean over and kiss Dad's forehead.*) I love you, Daddy.

    Dad: I love you, too.

"It's Just Going to Be Me and Karen"
May 27, 2018

I called ahead of time to see if Dad might be up for an adventure today. He was up, I was told, and ready to hit the road.

When I got there he already had his sweater on and was moving towards the door. He had his new hearing device with him - but he told Amanda that it was "just going to be me and Karen and we just talk..." and left it with her. Amanda handed me the hearing device surreptitiously, though, and once I got in the car with Dad I gave it back to him, and he put it on.

Dad: Where are we going today?

Karen: Let's go towards the water.

Dad: Yeah. Our last drive was nice.

Karen: It's a gorgeous day.

Dad: Yeah. It is!

Karen: How are you feeling?

Dad: What?

Karen: Are you comfortable?

Dad: I am what you see. I'm doing well.

(*We go to the Sisters Espresso for Dad's root beer float, but it's closed.*)

Dad: Is it closed?

Karen: I think so. (*I see Brooke, the owner, cleaning up on the side of the stand and ask her if the stand is closed. She says it is, but she can make a root beer float for anyone who might happen to be over 99. Bless her heart. I hand Dad his root beer float and let Dad know that Brooke made it especially for him.*)

Dad: Good! Thank you!

(*Dad points his finger to the right, indicating that's where he wants me to drive now. So I go right. We make a loop around the block and head back to the Sisters Espresso - I plan to head to the water from there.*)

Dad: (*Observing.*) We're heading back to where we were.

Karen: Yup. And then we're going to head west towards the water.

As we head up towards Bay View Park...

Karen: I love you.

Dad: What?

Karen: I love you.

Dad: No, I love YOU!

(*We both start laughing.*)

Dad: I wonder if the Annens' old cabin is still there?

Karen: I've never been to the Annens' cabin. I'm not sure where it would be.

Dad: It's near Warren Beach. I used to visit them when I worked at the Big Four Inn.

Karen: I haven't seen the Annens for a long time. They're probably not alive anymore...

Dad: (Laug*hing ruefully.*) No. They're gone.

(*We turn into Bayview State Park and I park facing out towards Anacortes.*)

Dad: Have you ever been to Anacortes?

Karen: Yes.

Dad: Is it a picturesque town?

Karen: Yes, it is. (*I don't tell Dad this - but he has been to Anacortes, too.*)

I roll down the windows and we smell the sea air for a while, and then we head back out of the park. As we head west I point to a peak rising through the haze...

Karen: Is that Whitehorse?

Dad: Yeah. Or maybe the Three Sisters. And there's Baker... did you ever climb Mount Baker?

Karen: Yes. I climbed it with you.

Dad: I can't remember the circumstances...

Karen: We climbed it with some teaching friends of mine, and Scotty...

Dad: That's right. Scotty was there, too.

Karen: (*Pointing to Baker.*) Yup. We all stood on that summit together.

I bring Dad back to his home.

Karen: I enjoy these drives with you.

Dad: I enjoy them, too.
Karen: I love you, Daddy.
Dad: I love you.

Dad gets out of the car and as he's closing the door he sees the magnet I've put on the outside of the passenger door. It reads, "God bless the whole world. No exceptions." Dad taps it with his finger, and says, "I like that." I tell him I like it, too. I help Dad into the house and he heads for the bathroom.

"I'm Taking a Break from Golf"
June 4, 2018

Dad is sitting at the dining room table, resting his forehead in his hand. He looks to be taking a little nap, sitting up. I stroke the top of his head and he opens his eyes.

Karen: Hi, Daddy!

Dad: Oh! Karen! I was just taking a break in my golf game. I got in six holes out of eighteen.

Karen: Yeah. You need a nap. (*I pull out a scrap of newspaper from his shirt pocket and unfold it. It's about a race car driver. This afternoon is full of surprises. I never thought of Dad as a golfer, and I never knew he was interested in race car driving.*)

Dad: (*Looking at the scrap of newspaper.*) That's about golf. Or. No, that one's about a race car driver.

Karen: (*I nod my head.*)

Dad: I took a shower today. (*Later I learn that he actually got up and went in and gave himself a shower.*) The ladies here help me. I've gotten so used to it that it doesn't bother me anymore.

Karen: Yup. They're here to help you with stuff like that. (*Counting days in my head.*) In two weeks we're going to take you up to Mount Rainier to celebrate your birthday.

Dad: Yeah. I won't have to drive this time. Someone else will take me up there. It'll be nice not to drive. (*I know Dad would love to get behind the wheel of a car again - so I appreciate his attempt to make me believe he's happy about being chauffeured.*) Are you off to work now?

Karen: No, I'm coming home from work. I thought I'd stop by and see you. I've got to get home and walk the dog and feed the cats now. But I wanted to stop in and tell you I love you.

Dad: I love you. See you soon.

"I Could Do Better Than That!"
June 8, 2018

Dad is sitting at the table drinking orange juice when I get there. He introduces me to Lola, a new resident and friend. Then he finishes his orange juice and heads out to the car with me. He has a doctor's appointment.

Dad: (*As we're driving to the appointment.*) How long have I been going to this eye doctor?

Karen: Since last August. Last month they saw that your eye had gotten worse and so they're going to inject medicine into it every month.

Dad: (*Pause.*) I didn't hear any of that.

Karen: Okay. (*I pat his knee.*) Never mind.

(*We drive a little further, then...*)

Dad: How long has Mom been gone?

Karen: (*It appears that today Dad remembers Mom is gone.*) She's been gone a year ago February. (*I glance over at Dad.*) Did you hear that?

Dad: No.

Karen: Okay. (*I decide to answer all his questions when we get to the doctor's office.*)

We pull into the parking lot and I find a place to park near the doctor's office door. I turn and talk directly into Dad's ear.

Karen: You've been going to this doctor since August. Last month they found your eye was getting worse and now they put medicine in your eye every month to make it better. (*Dad nods his head in acknowledgement.*) Mom has been gone for more than a year now. She passed away a year ago in February. (*Dad's head drops and he closes his eyes.*) Sometimes you remember Mom's gone and sometimes you don't. It's been traumatic for you. (*Dad nods his head.*) I feel Mom still with us, though. She loves you very much. She told me that.

Dad: (*Nods his head.*) I love you.

Karen: I love you, too.

I go into the office and let them know we're here, and then go back out to the car to wait with Dad. In a few minutes the receptionist comes to the lobby door and opens it for us - indicating it's time to come in. They lead Dad through the waiting area and right into an examining room. I talk directly into Dad's ear to let him know what they want him to do - "Look straight ahead. Good. Now look up. They're going to take your blood pressure now. Uncross your ankles. Cover your left eye. Cover your right. Good."

Dad: How'd I do?

Karen: You did great! (*I give a "thumbs up."*)

The woman who gave Dad his initial examination leads him back to an inner waiting room. I grab a *National Geographic* off a table there and hand it to Dad. It has a picture of an artist's rendering of a face on the cover. Without looking at the title of the article, I'm guessing it's a Picasso.

Dad: What's that?

Karen: It's a face.

Dad: Who did this?

Karen: (*I look at the title now, and see that it was, indeed, done by Picasso. I point out Picasso's name to Dad on the cover.*) Picasso.

Dad: (*Grunts.*) Picasso. I could do better than this. (*I'm cracking up.*)

We go into another examination room, and, after some photos are taken of Dad's eyes, we go to a third room. An assistant comes in. She looks at Dad's chart and notes that he'll be 100 in a couple weeks - she thinks this is cool. She tells us the doctor will be in soon and leaves. I look at Dad sitting across the room from me in the examination chair. He looks... fragile. And noble. His eyes have an expression of weariness in them. But there's courage in them, too. And kindness. My heart is filled with tenderness for him.

Karen: (*Mouthing the words.*) I love you.

Dad: (*Mouthing the words back.*) I love you.

(*Dr. Sapenstein enters the room.*)

Karen: (*Into Dad's ear...*) Dad, your doctor is Dr. Sapenstein. He's a climber, too. He climbed up to Muir with your friend who climbed to Muir every week - the woman in her nineties - I don't remember her name. (*Dad nods and smiles.*)

Karen: (*To Dr. Sapenstein.*) Okay, Dad's happy now. He knows he's with another climber.

(*Dr. Sapenstein smiles and shares that he looked Dad up on the internet and found all kinds of stories about him and his mountaineering adventures. Dr. Sapenstein is the perfect doctor for Dad.*)

The process of injecting medicine into Dad's eye is pretty quick, and we're soon headed out to the car.

Dad: (*Back in the car.*) Where are we going now?

Karen: (*Originally I'd just planned to take Dad back to his home, but seeing as how he asked...*) Let's go get you a root beer float.

(*I head to the Sister's Espresso for Dad's root beer float. Dad and I are both quiet. Every now and then I glance at him. He appears to be napping. I stop at the espresso stand and get him a float and bring it back to him. He thanks me and starts guzzling.*)

Back at his home now, I help him out of the car, into the house, and onto his recliner in front of the TV. He settles into it and I hand him the rest of his root beer float.

Karen: I love you, Daddy.

Dad: I love you, too. Happy New Year!

Karen: (*Laughing.*) Happy New Year!

"I Just Realized Mom Was Gone"
June 17, 2018

Dad is eating breakfast when Scott and I get there. I hand him a batch of birthday cards he's received from friends and family in the last week or two, and he tells me about each person who sent the card: This one went on a field trip with him once; that one worked with his brother; this one was the wife of a dear old friend; and that one came from the widow of another old friend. Each card brings him a smile and a happy memory.

Dad: I never dreamed I'd live to be 100. The days just keep coming. They just keep rolling by.

He says he just realized yesterday that Mom is gone, and he begins tearing up. I tell him that sometimes he remembers and sometimes he doesn't - and that I know it's been very hard for him. I tell him I'd probably want to forget that she was gone, too, if I was him. I tell him Mom loved him very much, and that they'd been able to say good-bye at the hospital - and he nods his head and wipes the tears from his eyes.

After he finishes breakfast we load him up in the car for a drive and head towards Sedro-Woolley.

Dad: (*Looking out the window at all the flags that are being put up to celebrate the Fourth of July.*) My mom was born on Flag Day. Her birthday was a week before mine. She died young. I can't remember how old she was now - I think in her fifties.

Soon Dad's head drops onto his chest. He's taking a nap. Scotty continues driving on the backroads of Skagit County while I snap pictures of barns, and Dad takes his nap. Eventually Scotty turns the car around and we head back to Dad's place. As we approach his home, I squeeze Dad's shoulders from the back seat. Dad reaches up his hand and motions for me to hold it. I grab his hand and squeeze it and he squeezes back. We hold hands until the car stops in front of the door. He opens the car door and I come around to help him out of the car.

Karen: I want to get a photo of my two favorite fathers.

(Scott and Dad move close together so I can snap their picture.)

Karen: I love you, Daddy.

Dad: I love you, Karen.

(Note: I don't remember ever hearing about Flag Day until Dad mentioned it today. When I googled it I discovered that Flag Day IS a week before Dad's birthday. Dad knows what he's talking about.)

Second Summer

In this memory I am 40 - almost 41. Dad is 79. Dad and I are climbing Mount Adams (the second highest mountain in Washington) with Scott and some friends. We get to about 10,000' when Dad stops. "I'm going to stay here," he says. "I'm holding you all back."

He is not holding ME back. I like his pace. But he lets me know he's done and we're going to need to go on without him. Our party continues on and reaches the top of Adams a few hours later. Adams will be the first big mountain I ever summit without Dad.

As we come glissading down from the summit Dad hustles up to meet us. "I've never been the one to sit and wait at base camp before," he says. "I don't like the worry of it." And he reaches out and hugs me.

Adams will be the last big mountain I ever climb.

"I Feel Like I'm in a Reality Show"
June 21, 2018

There's a film-maker at Dad's home to capture his 100th birthday celebration. Eric and his cameraman, Chip, are waiting for me when I arrive to visit Dad. They want to film me walking into Dad's home - and I'm thinking, "Oh, this is good - my big old 61 year-old backside is someday going to be seen in indy theatres across the nation. Why couldn't this have happened 20 years ago?" Because - I am embarrassed to admit - this is sometimes how my mind works. I have some vanity issues. But I go through the door again for them, and go into the home to find Dad at the table finishing up his breakfast.

Karen: We're heading up to Rainier tomorrow. We're going to see your mountain again.

Dad: It's not my mountain. It belongs to anyone who loves mountains.

Karen: (*Smiling.*) Tomorrow we'll drive up to the Beech House in Ashford. And then on Saturday we'll go up to Paradise.

Dad: We're going to the Beech House?

Karen: Yes. It's Jimmy Beech's old house. Remember your old friend Jimmy Beech? He took me on my first plane ride. He took us on a plane ride around Mount Rainier. We got really close to the glaciers...

Dad: (*Nodding, remembering.*) Is Jimmy still alive?

Karen: No. He's gone now. But Rick and Jana Johnson have remodeled his old house and that's where we'll be staying this weekend. And on Saturday we'll go up to Paradise.

Dad: (*Nods his head.*) What day is today?

Karen: Today is your 100th birthday. Today is Thursday. So in two days you'll be back at Paradise.

Dad: I don't want to climb the mountain again, though.

Karen: (*Laughing.*) No, you don't have to climb it. If you want you can just stay right in the car and look at your mountain from there.

Dad: Maybe just to Alta Vista.

Karen: (*Smiling.*) Okay. Maybe Alta Vista.

The phone rings and it's Dad's old mountaineering friend, Tom Hornbein, calling to wish him a happy 100th birthday. We put Tom on speaker phone so we can all hear him. Tom asks if anyone has an I-phone so we can get a live picture of him as he and Dad talk. The cameraman, Chip, pulls out his I-phone and they rig things up so we can see Tom and he can see Dad as they converse. Dad and Tom talk for a while about old friends, and what it feels like for Dad to be turning 100 (Dad says it doesn't feel any different than yesterday). I've moved to the back so the film-makers can catch the conversation on camera, but as the conversation comes to an end I hear Tom say, "Bye, Dee." And there's something about the way Tom says this - something very sweet and dear - that has me tearing up.

Scott and Andrew, and Dad's friend, Bob Ader, arrive to celebrate Dad's birthday. Andrew arm wrestles his grandpa at the dining room table. It ends in a tie, with both of them grinning at each other.

Eric and Chip follow Dad back into his room so they can share some old 8 mm movies Dad shot years ago and that they've digitalized for him. I can see that Dad is enjoying watching the old films.

Eric knows we're taking Dad up to Paradise on Saturday and he says he needs to capture every moment of the ride to Paradise. He plans to bring his camera into the car with Dad and my family as we make the drive from Ashford to Dad's old stomping grounds. This is not what I'd envisioned when I'd imagined the drive with Dad to Paradise - I'd been expecting my family to have Dad all to ourselves in the car - imagined myself leaning forward from the back seat to observe Dad's reaction when he sees his mountain again. It was not going to be the same sharing the back seat with Eric and his camera.

At the end of the birthday celebration...
Karen: Do you want to go for a drive now?
Dad: (*Nods head.*) Yes.

Karen: Where's your alpine hat? (*I look around the room and see it capping a lamp - which strikes me as something I might see in a college dorm room.*) Oh! There it is! (*I fetch it and clap it on Dad's head and we head out to the car.*)

Andrew and Dad's friend, Bob, get into the back seat. Today they're going to join us on our adventure. Chip follows Dad with his lens as Dad gets himself in the car. I close Dad's door and come around to my side of the car.

Dad: (*His eyes on the camera.*) I feel like I'm in a reality show.

Karen to Chip: (*Laughing.*) Dad says he feels like he's in a reality show. (*Chip laughs.*) Do you want to come with us?

(*Chip would like to go with us and goes off to confer with Eric, the film-maker. When he comes back he squeezes into the back seat with Andrew and Bob. I look back at these three full-grown men and start cracking up. Their knees are up to their chins; their shoulders are over-lapping. They are wedged in there like... well, like three grown men in the back seat of a Ford Fiesta.*)

Andrew: (*Grinning.*) It feels like we're in a clown car.

Dad: Are we going to Sunrise today? (*Dad has just been looking at footage he took of Mount Rainier years ago and is back in the national park in his mind.*)

Karen: No. We'll head to Rainier this weekend. But today I thought we'd head for the water. (*Raising my voice to talk to the wedgees in the back.*) We're going to take Dad to get his root beer float at the espresso we always go to.

(*We maneuver our way through the town and soon we're on Chuckanut Drive.*)

Andrew: Does Dee like the mountains better than the ocean? He mostly talks about the mountains.

Karen: (*To Dad.*) Do you like the ocean?

Dad: (*Nods.*) Yeah, I do.

Karen: (*To the wedgees in the back seat...*) I remember once when Dad and I were on a hike - we were on a mountain ridge - Dad asked me what song most inspired me. I was in my twenties and *Star Wars* had just come out and I think I said *The Star Wars* theme song or something. I asked Dad what song most inspired him and he said *The Lone Prairie* - and it was... here we were standing on a mountain ridge together and he said that *The Lone Prairie* most inspired him. It was weird and kind of cool. And then he sang it for me. He sang it like he was a little kid singing for his mom - it was very sweet and natural. (*Thinking.*) I think Dad likes being places where he has a broad view - on top of a mountain or in a prairie that goes to the horizon. (*Looking around at the flat Skagit farmland.*) Dad, do you like this area?

Dad: (*Nodding his head.*) Yes. The Skagit Delta. There were glaciers here once.

We drive to the Sisters Espresso and get Dad his root beer float. We head towards the water. We drive through Edison and talk to Chip a bit about how he came to be a documentary photographer. He tells us a little about himself - majoring in Latin American and Caribbean Studies; finding joy in photography; teaching photography for a year in Argentina; driving with his brother from Argentina to Central America and then selling their car and going to Costa Rica where they learned how to surf; and then from there to China. China?! Yes, from Costa Rica to China, where he lived for three years.

Karen: (*Grinning.*) Well, Chip, it sounds like you fit right in with Dad's community of family and friends.

We head back to Dad's home now. When we pull into the driveway he knows right where he is and opens the door to get out of the car. We help him back into the house.

Karen: I love you.

Dad: I love you.

(*Andrew gives his grandfather a hug. Bob and Dad hug and Bob tells Dad he'll see him again on the way to Rainier this weekend.*)

"Let's Go to Longmire!"
June 22, 2018

Karen: Are you ready to go to Rainier?
Dad: (*Nodding.*) I'm starting my second hundred years.

We help Dad into his care-giver's car. I lean through the car window and explain to Dad that we'll be in the car right in front of him. He nods his head in understanding. "We're going up to Ashford today," I remind him, "and then tomorrow we'll drive up to Paradise and you'll be on your mountain again." I kiss his cheek.
Karen: I love you, Daddy.
Dad: I love you, Karen.

We ride in a caravan to Rainier: Scott and I in the first car; Gwen, Gwen's grandson, Aiden, and Dad in the second car; Bob Ader and Xander in the third car. We're anticipating that we'll need to negotiate huge traffic jams through Seattle, but somehow we manage to maneuver around the mess and soon we find ourselves past the metro congestion and driving on country highways through green farmland, headed towards Ashford.

About an hour outside of Ashford I get a text from David, letting me know that Kristianne Schoening (whose father, Pete Schoening, had saved my dad and four others with his famous belay on K2) and her nephew and his family were at the Beech House. They'd thought the potluck party was today and had come a day early. I text my brother back to tell him we'll be there in an hour and that we have Bob Ader with us. Dave texts, "Oh! Kristianne was hoping to see Bob again! I'll let her know."

It has been an overcast day with no sign of Rainier. But now, as we near "Dad's Mountain" the clouds start breaking up and we begin to see patches of Rainier's glaciered slopes. I'm thinking, "Of course the mountain is revealing herself! She wouldn't stay hidden from Dad!" And I begin to think about the possibility of maybe getting Dad into the park and up to Longmire *today* to see his mountain - if he's up for it. I mean - why wait, right? The film-maker can still ride with us up to Paradise on Saturday - but maybe today we can sneak in a quick drive to Longmire with Dad - and Xander, Scott and I can have him to ourselves in the car for that precious moment when he sees Rainier again up-close.

When we get to Ashford I suggest to Scott that we stop at Rick and Jana's pottery shop before going to the Beech House. There we run into Kristianne and her nephew, Gabriel, Gabriel's wife, Terese, and their baby daughter. Gwen pulls her car in next to us and Bob parks his car a few spaces down.

Gwen: (*Smiling.*)Your dad was so excited when he saw the glimpse of the mountain. He was crying. He doesn't want to stop here. He wants to go all the way up to Paradise right now.

Karen: Let's do it! We don't have time to go up to Paradise - but let's go up to Longmire!

We confer with the Schoening family, Scott, Xander, Bob, and Dave, and we decide to go for it! The Schoenings had been up to Paradise earlier in the day, but couldn't see the mountain for the clouds. They're ready to give it another go.

We stop first at the Beech House to drop off our bags, and then pile into three cars and head for Longmire.

Dad is in the car with Scott and Xander and I. He's sitting in the front seat and I'm sitting behind him. This is how I'd originally imagined it would be. I lean forward and put my hand on his shoulder and Dad reaches up and squeezes my hand. In that moment I am completely happy.

We travel to Longmire, park the car, and help Dad to a bench where he can see his mountain. There's a small tree in his line of vision, but Dad really needs to sit and rest for a while, tree or no tree. His eyes are fastened on Rainier. He begins to describe the routes he's taken up its slopes, pointing with his finger.

Karen: It's been a while since you've been up here. How long has it been?

Dad: (*Thinking.*) Yeah. It's been a few years.

Karen: It's good to see it again, isn't it?

Dad: Yeeaah. (*He stretches the word out so it sounds like three syllables.*)

After a while my husband moves a chair off the Longmire Inn's porch and sets it out in the open, facing Rainier - there are no obstacles to a full line of sight of Rainier from that chair. We help Dad towards the chair, but when he's about three yards out from it he says he can get to the chair on his own. I instinctively reach out to help him, but Gwen (wisely) shakes her head at me and says, "He can do this." And we watch Dad climb another mountain as he makes it to the seat and settles into it.

Dad crosses his legs and makes himself comfortable in the chair. Aidan brings Dad an ice cream cone. He is surrounded by family and old friends, and Rainier is full in front of him. Life does not get any better than this. It is momentous.

After a morning spent in the clouds, the Schoenings are able to see Rainier now. I'm thinking they were meant to come today.

A tanned and spry woman - in her eighties maybe - approaches me and introduces herself. Her name is Annemarie and she's a climber and she'd heard from our mutual friend, Rick Johnson, that Dad would be coming up to Paradise tomorrow and she was afraid she'd miss him. So to see him NOW - right in front of her in Longmire - is like a miracle to her. She's clutching Dad's book, *The Challenge of Rainier*, and she's wondering if he would sign it for her. I give her a hug and take the book to Dad.

I explain to Dad who Annemarie is - write her name down on a piece of paper so he can see how it's spelled - and he autographs the book for her. He's an old hand at this kind of thing. He has just made Annemarie's day.

We stay at Longmire for maybe twenty minutes - and then it is time to go back down to the Beech House. It has been a long day for Dad. And tomorrow we're going up to Paradise!

Escort to Paradise
June 23, 2018

Ranger Rick Lorenz appears at the door at 10:30 to escort Dad and the caravan up to Paradise in Mount Rainier National Park. Dad finishes his breakfast and we sort everyone into cars to follow Rick into the park.

Dad is sitting in the front passenger seat so his vision is clear to take in everything around him. Xander, the cameraman, and I sit in the back seat. Scott is driving.

It's cloudy, but we're hoping that when we get to Paradise we'll be above the clouds and Dad will be able to see The Mountain.

Our caravan moves along the road to Paradise quickly and soon we arrive at the parking lot. A sign reads "PARKING LOT FULL" - but Rick leads us past the sign and takes us to a spot that's been especially reserved for our car and the other five cars in the caravan. Dan Jones, another ranger, is there waiting to greet us. Dad and Dan exchange handshakes through the car window, and Dan tells Dad that it is his honor to meet him. I get out of the car to help Dad out of the passenger seat and look up to see a dozen or more people standing in front of us, cameras at the ready. It appears Dad is an event.

As I help Dad out of the car the cameras start clicking. Most of these people appear to be tourists who just happened to be at Paradise when we arrived. I'm guessing most of them don't know who Dad is or what's really going on here - but they know that SOMEthing is happening and they want to make sure to capture the whatever-it-is in their cameras. I move forward to meet a few of them. I introduce myself and am introduced, in turn, to Satya, Krishna, and Pagma. The three are from North Carolina by way of India. As I guessed, they're not sure what's happening here, but they know it's something - so I explain to them that my Dad used to be a guide up here - that he's climbed the mountain more than fifty times - and that he's up here to celebrate his 100th birthday. They nod and smile and let me take THEIR picture. I have made three new friends.

Dad doesn't want to sit in the wheelchair Gwen has brought - but once he sits in it he makes no complaints, and no effort to get out of it.

We wheel him down to the Paradise Inn and roll him inside. There is a crowd waiting for him inside. As we turn and wheel him towards the fireplace, two lines form on either side of his path. He is the beloved king returning to his castle.

Ken Foreman waits for Dad by the fireplace in his own wheelchair. The two clasp hands and tear up when they see each other again.

Dad's friends and family gather around and sing happy birthday to him, and then come up in ones and twos and threes to greet him in the wheelchair.

But Dad doesn't want to stay there. At some point he gets himself out of the chair and starts to head for the doors to the outside. I come to one side, and someone else comes to his other side. "Where are you going, Daddy?" I ask, curious.

He gestures in front of him, and - with my support and the support of the person on the other side - he makes his way to a bench and sits down, facing where the mountain would be in his sight if there were no clouds.

"The mountain would be there," I say, pointing.

"I know!" he says, in disbelief that I would think he doesn't know that, and I start laughing.

Soon everyone else has joined us outside, and then people take turns sitting next to Dad for pictures.

After about an hour I feel it's time to take Daddy back down to Ashford. I'm sorry that he isn't going to see his mountain today - and even gladder that we were able to get him up to Longmire to see his mountain yesterday.

Back at the Beech House the place is packed with people! World-class climbers like Jim Wickwire, Craig Van Hoy, Bill Sumner, and the Whittaker twins are there - and cousins and old family friends that I haven't seen for years. Dad remembers every person who comes up to greet him. He shakes their hands, spends time talking to each person who approaches him. It is lovely to see him with his community again.

We eat, drink, sing happy birthday to him again, mingle, share stories. I am spinning. Literally. So many people to talk to - and so little time!

It has been a long day for Daddy. He is tired now. I ask him if he's ready for a nap, and he nods his head and says yes. I help him up and announce to his fans that he's going to take a nap now. Everyone wishes him a good sleep, and Gwen brings him into his room to get him ready for bed.

Tracy Spring, a gifted musician and daughter of Dad's old friend, Bob Spring, asks if she might come in when he's ready and sing him to sleep. When Dad's tucked into bed Gwen comes out and lets us know Dad's ready - and Tracy and I go into his room. I probably need Tracy's sweet and soothing music as much as Daddy does at this point. It's peaceful in the room. Dad's eyes are already closed. We turn off the lights and Tracy sits on a chair, her guitar on her lap, and sings softly to Daddy, "I'm just a little stone in the river..."

I close my eyes and let Tracy's music and words fill every crack and nook in my soul. It is a precious few minutes in the dark with Tracy's music and my father sleeping quietly in the bed. Tracy and I hug when she's done. It is a perfect way to send Dad off to his slumbers.

Eventually people start to say their good-byes and leave. What an epic day!

Reunion with Rainier!
June 24, 2018

I wake up and peek outside the curtains. There are blue skies out there!

My thoughts immediately turn to Dad. Yesterday he missed seeing Mount Rainier from Paradise because of the clouds. It would be a tragedy to get him this close to his mountain - knowing he'll probably never come back here - and not try to get him up to Paradise one more time to see Rainier up-close and personal.

I confer with Scott and Gwen, Dave, and Xander (whose birthday it is today) to see what they think. They all agree that if Dad's up for it, we should try to get him back up to Paradise. I ask Dad if he'd like to go back to Paradise today to see Rainier - and he nods his head and says yes. So it's a go!

Yesterday we had a ranger escort to Paradise. Today we won't. This means we need to leave early to beat the long line of cars that will soon start forming at the gate.

Dad's dear friend, the incomparable Jolene Unsoeld (a former state representative and widow of mountaineer Willy Unsoeld) and Jolene's son, Krag, join us at 9:00 and we let them in on our plans. They're happy to join us on our trip to Paradise.

Dad: But where is Mom in all of this? Will she be with us?

Karen: (*I have fielded this question so many times in the past - but, for some reason, I find myself at a loss today.*) No...

Krag: She'll be with us in her own way.

Dad: (*Looking confused.*) I don't understand. I didn't hear that.

Karen: (*Repeating Krag's fine answer.*) She'll be with us in her own way, Daddy. (*Changing the subject.*) Let's get you loaded up in the car.

The film crew left yesterday. Today's gathering in Paradise will be quieter and without fanfare.

The line is just starting to form at the gate when we get there - but it's not too bad, yet. We've put Dad in the car with Gwen so she can use his old Golden Passport - the national park pass that never expires, and that he bought when he first became a senior citizen. He's probably had it almost forty years.

The drive to Paradise is quick and without complications. Every now and then I look back to see if Dad is checking out the scenery from the car behind us. I can see that his head is up and he's awake. I smile, imagining him catching glimpses of Rainier through the trees.

When we get to the parking lot we see a sign that, like yesterday, tells us the lot is full. But we go through and find a place to park along the side of the road. As Gwen passes us we suggest to her that she use her adult family home's "handicapped parking" pass to find a place to park that's near the visitor's center for Dad. She moves on to find a spot, and my brother and Krag both park behind us on the side of the road.

When we get to Gwen's car Dad is complaining that she's using the handicapped parking pass. "No, we can't park here," he insists. "This is reserved!"

Karen: It's for you, Daddy. She can use the pass for you.

Dad: No. I don't need that.

Karen: It's okay, Daddy. Here - let's get you out of the car.

(Gwen brings Dad's walker around, but he doesn't want to use it. Then she brings up his wheelchair...)

Dad: No. I don't want that. I have friends up here. I don't want them to see me in that thing. (*Looking around.*) I need a bench to sit on.

Karen: (*Pointing to the wheelchair.*) You can sit in that for now. (*I roll the wheelchair up to him and he sinks into it.*)

Pretty soon Dave, and his daughter, Claire, her husband, Michael, Xander, Krag, and Jolene join us in a circle around Dad. We turn the wheelchair so he's facing the mountain. A man visiting from China is watching all of these proceedings and comes up to meet Dad. I tell him that Dad just turned 100 and is celebrating his birthday up here. He gets a look of awe on his face and gives Dad a little head bow to honor him. He wants to get his picture with Dad and we turn Dad around so that the mountain is behind the two of them and snap a picture for him. Then I get a picture of the two of them for myself.

Karen: Do you want me to turn you back around so you can see the mountain again?

Dad: It doesn't matter. I'm happy whichever direction I face.

(*This is a good answer, but I turn Dad around so he's facing Rainier. For a while we all enjoy the mountain together.*)

There's something I feel I need to say to Dad now. I know he was confused this morning when he asked about Mom. I know - from past experience with him - that he's not going to be satisfied with the vague answer we gave him. I don't want him to be wondering. I don't want him to think Mom has abandoned him...

Karen: Daddy, sometimes you remember and sometimes you forget - but... Mom passed on a year ago. You were able to say good bye to each other. She loved you very much.

Dad: Mom is gone?! I didn't know... (*He's choking up.*)

Karen: You knew, but then sometimes you forget. (*I point towards the mountain and tell Dad where we put Mom's ashes.*)

Dad: (*Nodding.*) Her ashes are up there...?

Karen: Yes. And she's with us right now. I feel her with us right now, smiling.

Dad: I'm glad you can feel her. (*He's quiet for a few minutes, thinking.*)

Michael and Claire go into the visitor's center. When they return five minutes later Michael is carrying a sign that he found in there. It's one of those signs with a little face cut out of it so people can stick their heads in there and get photos. The sign says: "Happy Birthday. 100. National Park Service." Apparently the National Park Service turned 100 a couple years ago, and this sign was made to celebrate the centennial of its creation. But right now the sign works perfectly for our needs and we show it to Dad, and then bring it down to him so that he can stick his face in the hole. We are all cracking up and snapping pictures. It is one of those perfect coincidences in life.

After a while we wheel Dad down to the Inn. He sits on the same bench he sat on yesterday, but this time he can see Mount Rainier.

The sun feels good on our faces. We're warm and drowsy and content.

We sit in the sun for maybe twenty minutes and then we all begin to stir at the same time. It's time to go back down the mountain.

As we're wheeling Dad back to the car - Dad rowing with the new walking stick Scott bought him, while Xander pushes the wheelchair from behind - we run into one of the rangers and get into conversation with him. He says that he was one of the people on duty for Dad yesterday, and it was his great honor to be part of it all. A few minutes later Rick - the ranger who escorted us up to Paradise yesterday - emerges from the ranger station to greet us. Then Brett - who coordinated the whole expedition to Paradise with me - comes out and introduces himself. I hug him and thank him for all he did to make yesterday work for Dad. He said he was happy to be able to do that for my father. It's the least they could do for him, he says. Dad is a legend up there.

I'm so grateful that I was able to meet Brett and some of the other rangers who helped us yesterday, and to thank them. Another happy coincidence.

We load Dad up in Gwen's car.

The rest of us head to our cars and start the trek back down the mountain.

When we get past the gate we see there's a long line of cars waiting to get in. The line stretches three miles long. We're glad we went up to the mountain when we did.

We're all feeling hungry now and turn into the parking lot of a Himalayan restaurant that Krag suggests to us.

Dad and Jolene sit across from each other at the table and the rest of us sort ourselves out into the rest of the chairs. We talk about mountains and Nepal and the Peace Corps and politics and old friends and music and Himalayan food. Tibetan prayer flags hang around us, gently wafting in the breeze. It is peaceful out there.

When we've finished lunch, we load Dad back in the car with Gwen.

Dad: (*Smiling and happy he had a chance to see his dear friend, Jolene, again.*) Did you meet Jolene?

Karen: Yes! I love Jolene! (*Kissing Dad's cheek...*) I love you, Daddy.

Dad: I love you, Karen.

"Vanilla!"
July 3, 2018

Karen: You're going to the dentist now.
Dad: Okay. (*Gets up behind his walker and starts heading to the car.*)
(*Well, THAT was easy!*)

When I made this appointment for Dad I forgot that this would be right when the Fourth of July Extravaganza would be happening in Sedro-Woolley. I circle the block a couple times before I finally find a parking space across the street from the dentist's office. I help Dad out of the car and grab the backpacks that have the official "Dad papers" in them. Dad gets behind his walker and we begin our journey across the crosswalk and to the other side of the street. Dad is not as quick as he once was and the cars are backing up. I smile and yell to the driver in the first car, "He's 100. Sorry!" The driver smiles back at me and gives us the thumbs up. She tells us to take our time - it's all good. The drivers behind her understand the situation and are all smiling at us.

When we're half-way across the street Craig Van Hoy suddenly appears behind us - a friendly grin on his face. He'd seen Dad from his mountain shop window and immediately recognized the hat. Craig was at Dad's big birthday bash at Rainier last weekend - and it's fun to see him now back in Sedro-Woolley. He and Dad exchange greetings and Craig helps Dad finish his journey across the street and to the dentist's office.

I get Dad situated in a chair while I fill out paper work for him, then I sit down next to him.
Karen: Do you remember Craig? He's a guide at Rainier...
Dad: (*Nodding.*) Yeah - and he was at the party last weekend.
Karen: That's right! He's pretty cool.
Dad: (*Nodding.*) Yeah, he is.

Pretty soon Misty calls us back into the room where she's going to work on Dad's teeth. Dad takes an immediate liking to Misty and calmly settles into the chair for the examination. He is very casual about all this. He crosses his legs at the ankles and folds his hands on his lap and awaits further events. Every now and then I yell directions from Misty into his ear, and he does whatever he needs to do for her.

Pretty soon Hansrolf comes in. Hansrolf cannot retire. Ever. He is irreplaceable. I do not know any other dentist who can make me laugh like he does. Basically, I go to him for the free stand-up comedy act he performs for me every year - the dental check-up is just a side thing.

Karen: (*To Hansrolf...*) What happened to all the cute pictures of puppies and kitties and bunnies you used to have in here? What's with all the posters of cavities and gum disease?

Hansrolf: We believe it's important to scare our patients.

(*His examination of Dad is quick and painless. He sees right away what needs attention and makes plans to fix things.*)

Hansrolf and Dad shake hands, and I gather Dad's things, put his hat back on his head, pay his bill, and direct him out the door and back across the crosswalk.

Dad: (*As we're driving back to his home...*) Where to next?

Karen: Where would you like to go?

Dad: Lunch.

Karen: Okay. I'll get you something... (*I head towards the Sisters Espresso for a cheeseburger for Dad.*)

Dad: (*Thinking.*) Thank you. Thank you for keeping track of my schedule for me.

Karen: You're welcome!

(*I pull into the Sisters Espresso and turn to look at Dad.*)

Dad: Vanilla.

(*I take this to mean Dad will have a vanilla milkshake. I go up and order a cheeseburger for him, and a vanilla milkshake. We just came from the dentist, but in my head I'm justifying a milkshake by thinking of all the calcium Dad's going to get from it. Listen. He's 100. What's the worst that's going to happen here? I hand Dad his milkshake and burger.*)

Dad: Thank you!

Karen: You're welcome!

(And then it's back to Dad's home. I help him out of the car and into the home.)

Karen: I love you, Daddy.

Dad: I love you, Karen.

"Good!"
July 4, 2018

Dad was in bed when I got there. Amanda told him that I was there to take him out for a bit, and he stirred and sat up. He looked up at me and smiled. He was ready to go!

(*On the drive to my home...*)
Karen: (*Pointing to the flags lining the road.*) It's the Fourth of July.

Dad: (*Nodding.*) I hardly notice holidays anymore. I've seen so many. Where are we going?

Karen: To my house.

Dad: To your house?

Karen: Yes. For the Fourth of July.

Dad: (*Nodding.*) Oh. (*Looking to the right.*) Oh! There's Baker!

Karen: Yes, the mountain's out today.

As soon as I park in the driveway, Dad's got his car door open and is getting out. I hurry around with his walker and help him up the ramp to our house.

We sit down to dinner around the table. Scott has prepared salmon and fills Dad's plate up. Dad and Andrew hug, and Dad asks his grandson what he's doing now.

Dad: Do you have a desk job?

Andrew: (*Laughing.*) Far from it.

Karen: (*To Andrew...*) I think he might be confused. The last he heard you were working as an engineer...

Andrew: Oh! Good point!

(*I fetch paper and pen so Dad and Andrew can communicate more easily.*)

Andrew writes: "I work at a restaurant. Two months ago I quit my job as an engineer."

Dad: What kind of engineer?

Andrew writes: "Mechanical aerospace."

(*Dad nods.*)

Andrew: I write poetry and perform at a theatre. Improvised comedy. Acting.

Dad: Do you read your poetry in a theater?

Andrew: (*Laughing.*) Not yet.

Karen: (*Into Dad's ear...*) Andrew and his friends have opened a couple times for Ryan Stiles - he's a well-known actor. And Andrew and his improv friends made a short film which showed at the Pickford in Bellingham.

Dad: (*To Andrew...*) Do you have humor in your improvisation?

Andrew writes: "Yes!"

Karen: I'm really proud of Andrew, Daddy. Life is so short - and Andrew doesn't want to waste one precious minute of it. He doesn't want to sit at a desk job. Not right now. He's got Molenaar in him.

Dad: (*Nodding and smiling.*) Good!

Karen: (*Laughing, and looking at Andrew.*) Well, there you have it. "Good!"

I find the Virgil's root beer four-pack that someone gave to Dad as a gift at Rainier last week. I kept forgetting to bring it to Dad, but now I pull one of the bottles out of the four-pack and give it to him to drink. Scott cuts him a piece of bumbleberry pie that he made from berries cultivated in the backyard, and that I picked on a hike last week. I top Dad's piece of pie off with ice cream. Dad is a happy camper. When he finishes his pie Dad announces that he's ready for a nap. It's time for him to go home now. I tell Dad how glad we are that he could join us today. I tell him we love him, and he says, "I love all of you!"

We put his baseball cap back on his head and load him up in the car to take him back to his home. Andrew and Scott give Dad hugs through the car window, and we're on our way.

(*As I'm driving him home...*)

Dad: I like going on these quiet, peaceful drives with you.

Karen: I do, too, Daddy. I do, too.

"What Choice Do I Have?"
July 9, 2018

Dad is stretched out on his bed when I get there. I lean in and say, "You've got a doctor's appointment now." I can tell he doesn't want to get up. But I reach out my hands and he takes hold of them and we get him in a sitting position. I put his shoes in front of him and he lets me pull them onto his feet. We try out the UW Alumni hat first - then I offer him his old alpine hat and ask him which hat he wants to wear today. He says he wants to wear his faithful old mountain hat. We load him in the car and away we go...

Dad: When do I get to stop going to doctor's appointments? I feel well now.

Karen: (patting his knee) I know. Doctor's appointments are no fun, are they? This one's to look at your teeth. You might have to have a couple teeth pulled.

(*Dad grunts. I can tell he is not happy about this.*)

Dad: It's handy that you live close to me and can take me on these errands. Thank you.

Karen: I'm glad to do this for you.

Dad: I keep forgetting I live almost to the Canadian border. I wonder how many of these people are Canadian. (*Looking out the window.*) You live near a lot of places - the supermarket, doctor's offices, museums, galleries.

Karen: Yeah. We don't have to travel far, do we?

We arrive at the doctor's office and get Dad situated in a chair in the waiting room while I fill out paperwork for him. Pretty soon we get called back for x-rays. But now Dad asks where "the urinal" is. This could be problematic. But I lead him to the restroom and close the door on him and send out a silent prayer that all will go well in there. Soon I hear the toilet flush and I hear his walker rolling across the restroom floor. I open the door to see him all put together and the restroom looking as pristine as it was when he went in there - and those of you with elderly fathers might appreciate the pride I felt in him at that moment.

The technician decides not to use the x-ray machine on him - the way it works she can see that it would end up smashing into his shoulders and she doesn't want to cause him any pain. So we by-pass the x-rays and go right into the room where the doctor will meet with him.

The doctor's assistant brings in a chair for me to sit on. This makes me really happy.

Karen: Look, Dad! I have a chair, too!

(*Dad grins and then starts laughing. His eyes are twinkling at me*.)

The doctor's assistant asks if Dad's ever had a joint replacement, and I say no - although a lot of his old climbing buddies have had hip and knee replacements. The doctor's assistant perks up and wants to know more about Dad's climbing. So we talk a bit about that, and then I say in Dad's ear, "You haven't had any joint replacements have you? But a lot of your climbing friends have had hip replacements and stuff..."

Dad: (*Smiling*.) I was easier on myself.

Dr. Kim asks Dad to open his mouth and I find myself opening my mouth wide in imitation. The doctor tells Dad to stick out his tongue and I find myself sticking out my tongue, too. Dad is observing Dr. Kim. After a moment he tells the doctor that he looks fit, and the doctor starts laughing, and makes some self-deprecating remark about his fitness. I mention that my Dad has climbed mountains on six of the seven continents, and the technician gets kind of excited about this and asks which continent Dad hasn't climbed on. I tell her Africa. He hasn't climbed Kilimanjaro.

The doctor is asking Dad questions and Dad says, "My hearing is shot." The doctor starts laughing. I like the way he is interacting with Dad - professional, but respectful and affable, too.

While the doctor is talking to the technician, I walk up to Dad and talk into his ear.

Karen: I'm really proud of you, Daddy. You're very brave. You're doing everything they ask you to do.

Dad: (*Shrugging and smiling*.) What choice do I have?

(*I start laughing with him. He has a point, I guess*.)

The doctor apprises us of the choices we have. At 100 years of age, extracting Dad's teeth is going to be really hard on him. We decide that, as long as Dad's not in any pain, we'll wait. I let the doctor know that I'm really relieved to hear this. My main concern for Dad is that he be comfortable.

Karen: (*Into Dad's ear...*) Daddy, are you in any pain?

Dad: (*Shaking his head no.*) No. I'm fine.

Karen: You could get surgery to have two of your teeth removed, or we could wait - not do surgery unless you feel pain. Do you want to not do the surgery?

Dad: No. I don't want the surgery.

And that was that.

I got Dad loaded back in the car. Just before I put the car in reverse, Dad asked, "How's Mom doing?"

Karen: (*Pause.*) Daddy, Mom's gone.

Dad: How long?

Karen: More than a year. (*I know Dad always worries about us when he finds out Mom is gone, so I address that.*) We're all okay, Daddy.

Dad: I always thought I'd go before her.

We pull out of the parking lot and head towards his home.

Dad:(*Thinking about the dentist he saw last week, and the doctor today.*) I like both my doctors.

Karen: They're good people, aren't they?

I decide to drive the backroads back to Dad's home.

Dad: There's Mount Baker. (*Thinking.*) Did we climb Baker together?

Karen: Yup.

Dad: I've climbed it a couple times, I think. But I can't remember the routes I went up.

Karen: I think when we climbed it we went by Kulshan Cabin.

Dad: Yeah. Did we stay in the cabin?

Karen: No. I think we slept on the slopes.

Dad: (*Nodding.*) Yeah.

As I approach the turn-off to Dad's home I find myself driving past it. I'm not ready to take him home, yet. I, of course, end up pulling into the Sister's Espresso. Dad makes a happy sound when he sees the familiar stop. This time Dad wants a vanilla milkshake.

Milkshake in his hand, I drive Dad back to his home. As I pull into the driveway he asks if someone's going to pick him up there. I tell him this is where he lives now.

Dad: Thank you for taking me to these appointments.
Karen: I'm glad I can do this for you. I love you, Daddy.
Dad: I love you.

"Sometimes I Go to These Quiet Places"
July 13, 2018

I bring Dad to my home to see if he wants to do some water-color painting today. On the way to my home we stop at the Sisters Espresso. I ask him what he'd like today. He says, "The usual." I ask him if he'd rather have a root beer float or a vanilla shake, and he opts for the shake. I found a watercolor he started earlier and have water, brushes, and paints laying out on the table for him when he arrives. He knows right where to go when he comes in the door.

He is quiet today. Pensive.

Karen: Are you alright, Daddy?

Dad: (*Nodding and leaning his forehead in his palm.*) Yes. Sometimes I just go to these quiet places to try to remember my trips.

I tell Daddy that a couple of his friends have told me Tony Streather (from the 1953 K2 Expedition) died - but that it turned out to be someone named Tony Strawther.

Dad: Tony was such a nice guy.

Karen: Tell me about Tony. When did you first meet him?

Dad: He was a lot more of a climber than we realized 'cause when we first contacted him we assumed he'd be somebody we'd have to teach along the way. But he was doing alright by himself.

(*After a while Dad closes his eyes and dozes where he sits.*)

Karen: Do you want to go home now?

Dad: What?

Karen: Do you want to go home and take a nap?

Dad: No.

Karen: Do you want to go out and sit in the sun for a while?

Dad: (*Nodding.*) That would be nice.

(*I help him negotiate his way out to the back deck and get him situated in a chair. I add root beer to his shake and bring out an album of his artwork for him to look at. He sips the root beer and looks through the album for a bit, and then he closes his eyes and takes a nap.*)

Karen: (*After about twenty minutes.*) I think it's time to get you home for a nap.

Dad: (*Nodding.*) Yeah.

I help him out to the car and lean over to buckle him into the seat. I give him a kiss on his cheek.

Dad: (*Smiling at me.*) I love you.

Karen: I love you, too, Daddy.

(*I come around and get in the driver's seat. Before I can start the car...*)

Dad: Where's Mom?

Karen: (*Pause.*) She's been gone for a year, Daddy.

Dad: She's been gone a year?

Karen: Yeah. (*Holding his hand.*) We're all okay. We're doing alright. She passed on peacefully in her sleep in our family room while I slept on the couch next to her bed. She loved you very much.

Dad: I hope she didn't suffer.

Karen: No. She didn't suffer. She died peacefully.

As I drive to I-5 I can feel Dad's mourning as he sits next to me. When I get on the freeway I reach over and grab his hand. He squeezes my hand, and I squeeze his hand back. Then he lets go of my hand so I can put both hands on the wheel.

I get him home and help him into the house.

Karen: I love you, Daddy.

Dad: I love you, Mo... (he starts to say "Mom")... Karen.

I give him a hug and he hugs me back. It is time for him to take his nap.

"I Don't Blame You"
July 16, 2018

Dad is sitting in his recliner in front of the television when I come in. He sees me and reaches out to give me a big, long hug.

He looks tired today. I ask him how he's doing, and he says he wishes he could "get out of here." I ask him if he wants to go for a drive, and he says yes.

Sometimes Dad is chatty on our drives, but today he isn't. Today he is reticent. He sits beside me quietly as we drive down Chuckanut. When I get to Sisters Espresso he asks for a vanilla shake. I drive to Bay View State Park, and he doesn't talk about the cows we pass, or the Padilla Bay Interpretive Center, or how he remembers being out here with me. I pull into the lot for Bay View State Park and park. I roll down the windows so we can smell the saltwater. I ask Dad if he likes being here and he says, "It's a nice park." But he is not enthusiastic.

As I'm returning to his home I point out Baker to him, and he nods and says, "Yeah." He keeps his eyes on Baker as we work our way through the flats and back to his home. I park in front of his front door...

Karen: I love you.

Dad: I don't blame you.

(*I look at him and see the twinkle in his eyes and start cracking up. He starts grinning then, too.*)

Karen: What's not to love, right?

(*Dad nods his head and smiles.*)

Megan and I help him up the stairs and let him take the lead. He passes the TV room. He passes the kitchen table. He heads to his bedroom for a nap. I tell him I'm going to let him take his nap now, and he says okay. I tell him, again, that I love him. He looks directly into my eyes and says, "I love you, Karen."

"But She Was Found"
July 20, 2018

Dad is just waking up at the dining room table when I come to pick him up for his appointment with the ophthalmologist. He isn't finished with his green juice - so I tell him he can bring it with him - and we load him up in the car.

The doctor's office lets us wait in the car until they're ready for us. Dad uses the time to take a nap. When they come out to get us I wake Daddy up and he follows the assistant into the office for his exam. Everyone knows Dad at the office now - and I always appreciate the kindness and courtesy they show him. He knows the pattern now, too - first this room for the exam, then that room to photograph his eyes, then the third room where he gets his treatment. As he's waiting for his eye injection I mouth the words, "I love you" and he mouths the words "I love you" back to me.

When Dad and I get back to the car I ask him if he wants to go for a drive now. He shrugs. He is tired. His eyes are closed - probably because they are dilated. The appointment has taken a lot out of him.

But I'm not ready to take him back home, yet. I get on I-5 and head to Conway.

His eyes are closed as we exit I-5 and start our drive through Fir Island. I tap his knee a couple times to tell him we are passing the cool Conway church, and some awesome barns - but he doesn't open his eyes. When I get a whiff of cow manure, though, I think that might wake him up - Dad was raised in dairy country in Orange County, California, and has always loved the smell of "dairy air." Sure enough. His eyes still closed, he breathes in deeply and says, "I smell cow shit." He is not unhappy about this.

I drive us to the Snow Goose Produce Market and ask Dad if he'd like an ice cream cone. He nods his head, so I go in to get one for him. When I hand him the cone he finally opens his eyes and perks up a little.

As I'm driving him back to his home I can't resist - I have to pull over to take a picture of a cool old barn. Dad asks me if I'm lost. I tell him no, I'm just exploring.

I try to stay off the main drag - it's really busy today - and go under an overpass and down some side roads and, finally, pull up in front of his house. He says, with some surprise, "You weren't lost at all, were you? You knew where we were the whole time. I thought you were lost."

Karen: No, I wasn't lost. I have a really good sense of direction. I've always had a really good sense of direction. I'm my Dad's daughter.

Dad: (*Nodding*.) Good.

Megan comes out to help Dad into the house. Dad isn't in a hurry to get out of the car. He needs a couple minutes to gather his energy. He says he needs to figure out where he is first. I tell him he's back at his home now, and he nods in acceptance.

Dad: (*To Megan...*) I thought Karen was lost. But she was found.

(*Megan starts laughing.*)

Dad: I had my directions all messed up today. Karen knew where she was.

(*I follow Dad into the house and to his recliner in front of the TV.*)

Karen: I love you, Daddy.

Dad: I love you. When will I see you again?

Karen: Soon. Probably in a couple days.

Dad: (*As I turn to leave...*) I love you.

Karen: I love you, too.

"I Finally Know Your Name"
July 22, 2018

I get a call that Dad is having a difficult time of it and wants to see me. He's remembered that Mom is gone and is grieving.

He is in the recliner in front of the television when I get there. His eyes light up at the sight of me. The first words out of his mouth are "I love you." I tell him I love him, too, and suggest to him that we move to a table where we can talk. He lets me hold his hand and help him to the table, and we get him hooked up to his hearing headset so he can better hear while we converse.

It has been a year and a half since Mom died. Dad had been in the hospital, suffering from delirium caused by a urinary tract infection, when Mom passed. When he was released from the hospital after her death, he never returned to the apartment they'd shared together before he went into the hospital. He, basically, woke up from his delirium to find himself in a new home and without his companion of 62 years. I know he's been working hard in the last 18 months to make some sense of it all. His courage since Mom's death has been awe-inspiring for me to witness. I always knew he was brave - his mountaineering adventures are proof of that - but I never realized the amazing depth of his quiet steely inner resolve until the last year and a half. I think I finally understand now how he survived those weeks on K2. I finally understand why so many people look on him as a hero. He is one. A genuine real life hero. And he's my father.

Now, for the first time since Mom died, I feel that Dad will be able to understand when I explain the sequence of events that brought him to his current home.

Dad: Mom is gone?
Karen: Yes.
Dad: Did she suffer?
Karen: No, she was being medicated for the pain.
Dad: How did it happen?
Karen: You and Mom were both in the hospital at the same time. She was on the floor above you. She had congestive heart

failure. You were on the floor below her with a urinary tract infection.

Dad: We were both in the hospital? I don't remember any of that. Why was I in the hospital?

Karen: For a urinary tract infection.

Dad: Oh. I don't remember.

Karen: You were delirious because of the infection.

Dad: (*Nodding.*) Oh.

Karen: I'm told that someone brought you up to her room in a wheelchair so you could say good bye. But I didn't get to see that.

Dad: I don't remember saying good bye to her.

Karen: No, your memory of that time is gone. (*Pause.*) When Mom was released we decided to bring her to my home to care for her. We thought we had months - but when they brought her to our home we realized that she was near the end. We spent the whole day telling each other we loved each other. She told me how much she loved you...

Dad: (*Tearing up.*) Was she in pain?

Karen: No, she was under medication. I was sleeping on the couch next to her bed when she passed. In my dreams I felt this joy and peace brush past me. When I woke up she looked to be sleeping quietly, and I started to go back to sleep... then I realized she was too still. I checked on her and she was gone. I went upstairs to Scotty and told him I thought Moz was gone and he came downstairs and checked her pulse, touched her - she was cold. He affirmed that she'd passed. But... I felt when she passed... I felt like she'd touched me with love and joy as she left...

Dad: (*Tearing up.*) Where was I?

Karen: You were still in the hospital. A doctor let us use her stethoscope to tell you Mom was gone - and you grieved, but the next day you didn't remember she'd passed. So then we sort of lied to you. You'd ask how Mom was doing and we'd say she was fine. But then I asked how YOU were doing and you said you'd be doing a lot better if we told you how Mom was doing. (*Dad laughs at himself - but there are tears in his eyes.*) I decided I needed to respect you by telling you the truth... but... it hurts you. When you forget that Mom is gone would you rather we tell you the truth or say she's fine...?

Dad: Tell me the truth.

Karen: You're very brave, Daddy. (*I give him a hug.*) And now we needed to figure out where to bring you when you were released. Before Mom died, your assisted living place told us they couldn't take you and Mom back. We only had a couple days to find a new home for Mom and you. That's why we brought Moz to our home. And when you were released - we didn't want to put you in some institution full of strangers...

Dad (*Shaking his head vehemently.*) No.

Karen: But I didn't have the know-how to take care of you in my home. You have memory problems (*I see the distressed look on his face and quickly reassure him*) - you're still brilliant and smart and wise and funny - and you have no problem remembering what happened forty or thirty years ago - but you have a hard time remembering yesterday or last week... I think when Mom passed that got worse for you. So we needed some place with people who knew how to take care of you and could love you like we do. The social workers at the hospital suggested we look into adult family homes and so I started calling around. The second place I called was this place...

Dad: This place where I am now?

Karen: Yes. Dave and I decided we'd check this place out. We decided if we didn't like the look of it we'd just drive right by. But there were bird feeders in the front yard, and cats and dogs, and... it felt like Moz had led us here for you.

Dad: (*Nodding and smiling.*) To this place?

Karen: Yes. I saw a rainbow that morning - and it seemed like a sign to me that everything was going to work out. And then we found this place and we met Gwen...

Dad: Who's Gwen?

Karen: Gwen's the woman who owns this place. She takes care of you. When we met her we found out she was related to your favorite author, John Muir, and that she likes the mountains, too. She and I took you up to Mount Baker last summer. And she came with us when we took you up to Rainier for your 100th birthday. Do you remember going up to Rainier for your 100th birthday? You had a ranger escort and they blocked off some parking spaces for you, and there was a camera crew making a documentary of you - it was epic!

Dad: No. I don't remember any of that.

Karen: I'll go get the pictures! (*I go into his bedroom and find the photo album of pictures from his 100th birthday weekend.*) See? Here you are arm wrestling with your grandson, Andrew. (*Dad smiles.*) And do you know who that is?

Dad: That's Bob Ader.

Karen: Yeah. He came all the way from Colorado to celebrate with you. And here you are at Longmire. There's Pete Schoening's grandson and great-granddaughter... and there's Kristianne Schoening - remember her? (*Dad nods.*) And see - there's Gwen!

Dad: (*By this time Gwen has joined us at the table. Dad looks up at her and recognizes her. He points to her and smiles.*) I finally know your name! (*Gwen starts grinning.*)

Karen: (*Pointing to a picture of Dad with his face in the photo hole of a sign.*) Michael, your granddaughter Claire's new husband, found this sign that had 100th birthday on it inside the Visitor's Center - it was to celebrate the National Park's centennial, but we thought it would be perfect for you, too. So we had you stick your head in there. (*Dad starts grinning.*)

Karen: Do you know who this is?

Dad: (*Nodding.*) That's your son. That's Alexander.

Karen: Yeah, he was up there with us. And there's Casey and his girlfriend... Oh! This was a special moment - do you recognize this person?

Dad: Kenny Foreman, my old Coast Guard buddy.

Karen: Yeah. You and Kenny held hands and sat next to each other in your wheelchairs. It was epic!

(*I start pointing out all the people who came to join Dad for his 100th birthday. Most of his old friends he recognizes - some he doesn't at first, but quickly remembers after a prompt.*)

Dad: (*Concerned.*) How was I? Did I carry on conversations...?

Karen: You were brilliant! You were smart and funny and wonderful!

Dad: (*Smiling with relief.*) Good.

Karen: Gwen's grandson was with us, too - here he is pushing you around in the wheelchair at Paradise. You didn't want to get in that wheelchair - you said you had friends up there and you didn't want them to see you in it. (*Dad starts laughing at himself.*) But you finally sat in it and let us roll you around.

After we go through the album I put it back in Dad's bedroom and ask him if he would like to go for a ride. He says yes. So we get his shoes on his feet and his hat on his head and load him up in my car.

Dad: Let's head for the beach.
Karen: Okay.

We drive through Burlington for a few minutes.
Dad: (*Thinking.*) I haven't seen Mom for about a year.
Karen: Daddy, she's gone.
Dad: Was there a service for her?
Karen: Yes.
Dad: Was I there?
Karen: Yes.
Dad: Did I speak at her service? Was I... alright?
Karen: No, you didn't speak. But you took care of us. You were wonderful.
Dad: Good.

We drive by Padilla Bay and then turn back to his home. Gwen comes to help us and I ask Dad if he remembers her. He nods and smiles and says, "Gwen." We bring him back to the recliner.

Dad: I love you!
Karen: I love you, too, Daddy!

"I'm So Proud to Have You for My Father!"
July 25, 2018

I stop by to see Dad. Amanda meets me at the door and says she was just about to call me - Dad is thinking he's going to a track meet today and he's waiting for someone to pick him up. She ask him if he is going to pole vault - and he tells her he's too old for that. But he's going to meet with some of his old track friends and watch a meet.

I get his hearing headset, the photo album that shows pictures from his 100th birthday party, and the photo album that shows pictures from Mom's memorial service, and go into the kitchen to talk to him. Lately I've had more confidence about carrying on an honest conversation with him than I have in the year before this. Maybe it's having the hearing headset - that helps a lot. Or maybe he seems more able and ready to hear about the challenges of the last year than he was before this. He's disoriented about time and place - but he's still intelligent and self-aware. He's shown me he's able to honestly evaluate himself and his situation. He's also shown me that he can recognize a lie when he hears it, and appreciates being told the truth.

Karen: Hi, Daddy? How are you doing?

Dad: I was looking for a little suitcase to put my things in. I'm waiting for somebody to pick me up and take me to the track meet

Karen: There's no track meet today.

Dad: (*Looking confused.*) I'm supposed to meet with some old track stars...here in Pullman...

Karen: You're in Burlington.

Dad: I'm not in Pullman?

Karen: No. But you were with some track stars for your 100th birthday celebration. (*I open up the photo album that has pictures from his centennial celebration.*) You maybe don't remember this... you've had some problems with your memory...

Dad: I don't have memory problems!(*He gestures to the photos in the album.*) I remember this.

Karen: You remember your 100th birthday? I'm so glad! (*We look through the pictures together - identifying old friends - including track star, Doris Brown, and her coach, Kenny Foreman. When we're done with that album, I open up the album to Moz's memorial celebration.*) I wanted to show you pictures from Moz's memorial celebration because you were asking about that during our last visit. (*I watch his face and see a shadow pass over it - I'm not sure he remembers.*) I'm not sure you remember... Moz passed...

Dad: (Maybe wanting to show me he doesn't have "memory problems.") I remember.

Karen: (*Pointing to one of the pictures.*) See? I used Moz's red cat shoes - I put them on the podium during the service...

Dad: Her what?

Karen: Her red cat shoes... remember those shoes?

Dad: (*Smiling and nodding.*) Yeah. Where are they now?

Karen: They're on my mantelpiece. (*Dad smiles.*) The service was held at the local Unitarian-Universalist fellowship. Do you know why?

Dad: (*Shakes his head.*) No. Why?

Karen: When you and Mom first moved up here I brought you to the UU fellowship because I was going to talk there. You looked at the program and wondered what my name was doing on it. (*Dad and I smile together.*) And Moz said, "I could have my memorial service here!" She liked the mountain tapestry at the front of the church. I didn't realize that she was going to be gone within the year. But when she passed I remembered what she'd said, and we had her celebration there.

Dad: (*Smiling and nodding.*) Oh. (*Pointing to the two photo albums.*) Can I keep these?

Karen: They're yours!

Dad: I need a little suitcase or something to put them in...

Karen: I'll just leave them next to your bed and you can look at them whenever you want. If you have a hard time remembering you can just look at the albums.

Dad: (*Nodding.*) Okay.

Karen: Would you like to go for a drive now?

Dad: I'm waiting for somebody to pick me up and take me to the track meet...

Karen: There's no track meet today. You're just a little confused...

Dad: (*Looking embarrassed.*) Oh. I thought there was a track meet...

Karen: No. You're just a little confused. But... that's understandable! (*I explain to Dad that this is the fourth home he's had in the last three years and that it's no wonder he's a little confused. We review what we talked about on our last visit - he and Mom being in the hospital at the same time; their assisted living place letting us know they couldn't come back once they were released from the hospital; bringing Moz to my home for hospice care; her passing early the next morning; finding this home for him in Burlington.*)

Dad: This is my home?

Karen: Yes. (*Tearing up.*) Daddy, I'm so proud you're my father! You're smart and wise and kind and funny.

Dad: (*Tearing up.*) I'm so proud to have you for my daughter.

Karen: Last weekend Scotty and I hiked up to the Skyline Divide...

Dad: I've been up there. I painted a few paintings up there.

Karen: Yes! You hiked up there with us one time. There's a 360 view up there (*Dad nods*) - Mount Baker, Mount Shuksan... and I was up there last weekend, looking at Baker, and thinking what a HUGE mountain it is and who did I think I was to climb it... and then I reminded myself I HAD climbed it - and that was because of you. You got me up that mountain and Rainier and Adams and Hood. I couldn't have climbed those mountains without you. You gave me the mountains. I'm so grateful to have you for my father!

Dad: I'm so grateful to have you for my daughter!

(*We cry and laugh and hold hands for a few minutes.*)

Karen: I love you, Daddy.

Dad: I love you, Karen.

"We're Neighbors Now!"
July 27, 2018

I stop in to see Dad. He's lying in bed watching TV when I get there.

Dad: It's my daughter!

Karen: Hi, Daddy!

Dad: We're neighbors now!

Karen: (*Hugging him.*) Yes, we are!

Dad: Are you dating anyone nice?

Karen: I'm married to Scotty.

Dad: Oh! You got a good one!

Karen: Yes, I did.

Dad: (*Smiling.*) He got a good one, too.

Karen: Thank you, Daddy. How are you feeling?

Dad: Good.

Karen: I just stopped in to say hi and tell you I love you.

Dad: That's all I need! I love you, too.

"I Don't Think She's Really Gone"
July 29, 2018

Dad is brilliant today!

Amanda sends word that he's up and feeling chipper. So I stop by to see if he'd like to go for a drive. He's finishing breakfast when I get there, but he soon has his alpine hat on his head and his shoes on his feet, and is moving (at a rapid pace) towards the door...

On the way out of town Dad asks me if I've ever been to the top of Burlington Hill. And then he says, "I've probably asked you that before, haven't I?" And when we pass a field with new crops planted, he asks me (again) what was planted there, and then says, "I've probably asked you that before, though, haven't I?" I get the sense that he realizes he has a memory problem, and that he's in the process of working to rebuild his memory. He is still pushing himself to climb mountains - still facing challenges head-on. He is my hero.

My original thought is that I'll swing by the Sisters Espresso for his shake and then take him up to Bayview State Park for a quiet sit on a bench. But on the way to Sisters Espresso Dad says he thinks he remembers a painting he has to finish at my home. So I get him his vanilla shake and then bring him to my house to see if he wants to work on his latest watercolor of Rainier.

He settles into a seat at the table. I pull out his paints, sponge, watercolors, brushes, and his latest watercolor project, and he sets to work.

He has his hearing headset on today, so we can have a conversation. His hearing headset makes all the difference. I have my camera with me and record some of our conversation. This is both a good thing and a bad thing. There are times when he says the most profound things - but I haven't been recording - so then he'll have to repeat himself for the recording. Sometimes there are things he says and does that are so precious to me I decide I don't want to remember them as a recording...

Karen: You're not a prejudiced person. You must have had good parents. Where you grew up - in Los Angeles - did you live in a part of town with people from a lot of different cultures and backgrounds? Was there racism where you lived?

Dad: There was racism in Los Angeles. (*Smiling.*) But we lived in the opposite part of Los Angeles. I grew up with mostly Japanese farmers. Most of my friends growing up were Japanese.

Karen: Daddy, tell me about the part of Los Angeles that you were raised in.

Dad: Are you recording this?

Karen: Yeah. Is that okay?

Dad: (*Nodding his head.*) Yeah. I lived in southwestern Los Angeles - which was mostly related to the Japanese truck farmers. We were kind of on the edge of the developed part of Los Angeles city, so we just walked a couple blocks and we were out in the fields.

Karen: Most of your friends were Japanese?

Dad: Yeah.

Karen: So you grew up in a place that didn't have a lot of prejudice?

Dad: Yeah. There are places that I've never had an interest in visiting because they are still very prejudiced and the Civil War is still in their blood.

(*I watch Dad paint for a while.*)

Karen: You're 100! That's crazy!

Dad: You tell anybody you've got a father 100 years old and they're going to think you're just...

Karen: Exaggerating?

Dad: Yeah.

Karen: When you paint do you know ahead of time what you're going to paint in the foreground?

Dad: (*Shaking his head.*) No.

Karen: So it just evolves?

Dad: Yeah.

Karen: What are you going to do with this one? What do you see?

Dad: Over here I'm going to paint some trees. And over here an island of trees. And up here a sub-ridge of the mountain. (*Thinking.*) You kind of want three points of interest, but not one dominating.

(Of course I haven't recorded any of Dad's thoughts on painting - so now I make him go through the whole conversation again. He is very patient with me.)

Karen: Daddy, I really love spending time with you.

Dad: *(Brings his head up and smiles and gives me the focused, penetrating look of someone who is really listening.)* I was going to say the same thing to you earlier. I love the drives we take together.

Karen: Were you the only artist in your family?

Dad: In my immediate family, you mean?

Karen: Were your grandparents artists? Were your parents artists?

Dad: No.

Karen: *(Laughing.)* How did that happen?

Dad: *(Thinking.)* I've always enjoyed drawing. And I enjoy drawing foregrounds for mountains.

Karen: What is your favorite place you've ever traveled?

Dad: Paradise Valley.

Karen: Wow! Mount Rainier. Was that better than the Alps?

Dad: Well, the Alps have more history...

Karen: But Paradise Valley is the best.

I watch Dad for a while, debating with myself if I should ask what I want to ask...

Karen: Daddy, I want to ask you a hard question...

Dad: Okay. I may give you a hard answer.

Karen: Do you think we'll see Mom again?

Dad: *(Thinking.)* I don't think Mom is really gone.

Karen: Do you feel her here?

Dad: *(Thinking.)* I wasn't surprised that she was gone. For the last year or two she talked about friends who had died, and I think she knew... I think she was trying to prepare me.

Karen: Yeah. I think she knew. When you were both in the hospital she didn't want to leave because she loved you and wanted to take care of you. You didn't want to leave because you wanted to take care of her.

Dad: *(Smiling sadly.)* I was shocked when you told me she was gone... but I wasn't surprised.

Karen: (*Feeling sad for him, and guilty, and unsure what I should do.*) Would you rather I not tell you Mom is gone when you forget? ...Was it bad of me to tell you?

Dad: (*Emphatically.*) No! You need to tell me. And I need to deal with it.

Karen: We carry Mom around in our memories of her, don't we? She's always with us.

Dad: (*Nodding.*) Yeah.

Karen: I'm glad we're neighbors, Daddy.

Dad: Yeah.

Karen: I love you.

Dad: I love you.

Dad is tired now. He'll come back and work on this painting another time. Right now it's time for his afternoon nap.

As I'm helping Dad get into the car, he turns and looks at me and reaches out to give me a hug. "I love you, Karen," he says.

I kiss him on the cheek. "I love you, too, Daddy."

I am a year old. Mom has dressed me in a pretty pink dress to greet Dad when he gets home from work. At some point between Moz buttoning me up in the dress and the arrival of Dad, I seem to have found a mud puddle. I am covered in muck. I'm waiting on the lawn when Dad pulls into the driveway. As I hurry towards the car, giddy to see him again, he pulls out his camera and snaps my picture. He is laughing. And then he's out of the car and I'm in his arms - mud and all. My hero is home.